HEART
OF THE
HOME

If in your house
this book you see
Please hurry!
Bring it back to me. ♥

"Go, little book, and wish to all
Flowers in the garden, meat in the hall,
A bin of wine, a spice of wit,
A house with lawns enclosing it,
A living river by the door,
A nightingale in the sycamore!"

♥ Robert Louis Stevenson ♥

HEART OF THE HOME

NOTES FROM A VINEYARD KITCHEN

BY SUSAN BRANCH

Little, Brown and Company
Boston · Toronto · London

Library of Congress Cataloging-in-Publication Data
Branch, Susan
    Heart of the home.

    1. Cookery.   2. Entertaining.   3. Home economics.
    I. Title
    TX715.B8175   1986   641.5   86-10312
    ISBN 0-316-10631-3
♥ Excerpt from "He Digs, He Dug, He Has Dug" by Ogden Nash reprinted by permission of Little, Brown and Company from Verses From 1929 On. Copyright 1949 by Ogden Nash.
♥ Caption from cartoon by E.B. White and Carl Rose reprinted by permission of The New Yorker. Copyright 1928, 1956 The New Yorker Magazine, Inc.
♥ Excerpt from Mainstays of Maine by Robert P. Tristram Coffin reprinted by permission of author's heirs. Copyright 1944 by The Macmillan Company.

♥ ♥ ♥

PRINTED IN THE UNITED STATES OF AMERICA

DEDICATION

There is nothing like a big family — I know it for I am the oldest of eight children & feel very lucky for it — we have more fun, more stories & more memories & forever we'll hang together. ♥ This book is dedicated to them: to my Grandma, who has always been the heart of our home; to my Dad, Jack, who worked so hard to make our life good & whose laugh we love to hear; to my Mom, Pat, who is pure sunshine & loved her little "dolls" so well; and to my brothers and sisters — the singingest, dancingest, funniest and happiest bunch of maniacs I know: Tim, Steve, Chuck, Brad, Paula, Mary and Shelly. ♥ I love you all.♥

♥ The Poppy is the California State Wildflower ♥

CONTENTS

"To Adam Paradise was home.
To the good among his descendants
home is paradise."

Hare

APPETIZERS

"To invite a person into your house is to take charge of his happiness for as long as he is under your roof." A. Brillat-Savarin ~ ♥

APPETIZER IDEAS

- Scoop out cherry tomatoes with melon-baller and fill with pesto, p. 79.

- Lay out slices of ham and spread with softened cream cheese with chives. Roll up and slice. Chill.

- Put cream cheese with chives on a Bremner wafer. Top with a fat slice of radish.

- Wrap seedless grapes with a mixture of cream cheese and Roquefort cheese. Roll in chopped nuts. Chill.

- Mix cream cheese with chives, and minced parsley, with chopped red pepper. Spread on toasted cocktail rye bread.

CHICKEN WINGS

325°   24 pieces

24 chicken "drumettes"
½ c. honey
2 Tbsp. Worcestershire sauce

⅓ c. soy sauce
1 clove garlic, minced
Juice of 2 lemons

If your market does not sell the "drumettes", buy a package of 12 chicken wings, remove the wing tips, and break each into two pieces. Preheat oven to 325°. Put the wings into a shallow baking dish. Mix remaining ingredients and pour over. Bake for 1 hour and serve warm.

NEW POTATOES

2 dozen tiniest new potatoes
½ c. sour cream
chopped chives
crumbled bacon (or caviar)

Cook the potatoes. Cut each in half and scoop out a small cavity with a melon-baller. Fill with sour cream, chives and bacon. ♥

ARTICHOKE DIP

Mix together:
1 jar artichoke hearts ~ drained and chopped
1 c. mayonnaise
1 c. Parmesan cheese

Bake at 350° for 30 minutes. Serve with hot French bread or pita. ♥

CHEESE BITES

Toast rounds of bread on one side and let cool. Mix together ½ c. mayonnaise, ½ c. Parmesan cheese and ¼ c. minced onion. Spread mixture on untoasted side of bread and broil till brown and bubbly. Serve hot. ♥

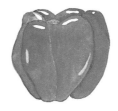

GRILLED PEPPERS
400°   Serves Six

A perfect barbecue appetizer, colorful & seasonal — but you can also cook them in the broiler when barbecuing isn't possible. ♥

3 large red bell peppers
Parsley Sauce (below) or Pesto (p.79)

Preheat oven to 400°. Bake the whole peppers for 10~15 min., turning once or twice, till black. Put them into a paper bag, close tightly; allow them to cool (this steams them). Rub off the skins, cut them in half lengthwise, remove seeds & cut them into thick strips. Thread the peppers on skewers & grill lightly (or broil). Arrange on platter, dribble over Parsley Sauce (or Pesto) and serve. ♥

Parsley Sauce

1 bunch parsley (1½ c.)	3 Tbsp. basil
6 cloves garlic	1 c. olive oil
4 Tbsp. lemon juice	pepper, to taste

Put all ingredients in food processor & purée. ♥ This sauce is also delicious on pasta. ♥

STEAMED CHINESE DUMPLINGS
Makes 20

You can serve these as hors d'oeuvres or alongside a salad for the first course of a Chinese dinner. ♥

      2 Tubes refrigerated dinner rolls
      1 lb. ground pork
      4 Tbsp. minced green onion
      3 Tbsp. soy sauce
      1 Tbsp. sesame oil
      ½ c. chopped water chestnuts
      freshly ground pepper
      ½ tsp. salt

Lay dinner rolls on lightly floured board ~ flatten with palm of hand then roll out with floured rolling pin till about 4" in diameter. Mix all other ingredients well. Put about 1½~2 Tbsp. pork mixture in the center of each round ~ gather up sides to meet in middle ~ twist top to close tightly. Put a damp cloth in the top part of vegetable steamer & put the dumplings on the cloth, 1" apart. Steam over boiling water for 20 min. Serve. ♥

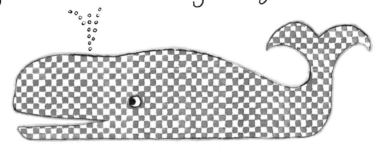

FRIED BRIE

This would also be wonderful served in a light lunch with cold Stuffed Artichokes (p. 54). ♥ Try crisp, tart apple slices as an accompaniment to the cheese. ♥

½ c. milk
2 Tbsp. heavy cream
1 lg. egg
½ wheel Brie cheese, chilled
3½ c. French bread crumbs, finely ground

1 tsp. coarsely ground pepper
1 Tbsp. minced parsley
⅛ tsp. thyme
Oil

Combine milk, cream & egg. Remove rind from Brie and cut into 6 slices. Dip each piece into milk mixture, and then coat thickly with bread crumbs, pepper, parsley & thyme (mixed together). Refrigerate coated cheese for 15 minutes. Remove from refrigerator, dip again in milk mixture, & coat once more with crumbs. Heat 2" oil in a large skillet over moderately high heat. Fry for a few seconds, till brown and crisp on both sides. Serve ♥.

"You two can be what you like, but since
I am the big fromage in this family, I prefer
to think of myself as the Gorgon Zola."
Ogden Nash ♥

CARPACCIO

Makes about 45

Don't be put off by the raw beef ~ this is an exciting hors d'oeuvre that will be snapped up in a second. ♥ Its imperative that you (or the butcher) slice the meat paper-thin; its easier if it's partially frozen. ♥

♥ 1¼ lbs. very lean top round steak
   Slice paper-thin
♥ 3 French bread baguettes
   Slice the bread in ¼" slices. Put them in a single layer on a cookie sheet & bake at 275° for 10 min. until dry. Cool & reserve.
♥ Tarragon Butter
   1 c. butter, softened
   2 Tbsp. tarragon, minced
   3 Tbsp. parsley, minced
   1 Tbsp. fresh lemon juice
   Cream all ingredients together & refrigerate.
♥ Carpaccio Sauce
   4 Tbsp. red onion, chopped   5 Tbsp. Dijon mustard
   3 garlic cloves   ¼ c. vinegar
   1 c. parsley, chopped   2 Tbsp. fresh lime juice
   4 anchovy filets   1 tsp. Worcestershire sauce
   10 cornichons (tiny French pickles) ¼ c. olive oil
   ½ c. capers   ¼ c. vegetable oil
   Put all ingredients except oil into food processor; whirl 20 seconds. Combine the olive & vegetable oils; with machine running, add oil in a very slow steady stream until thickened. Cover & refrigerate.
♥ To Serve
   Butter the bread. Cover each slice with a thin piece of meat & top with a little sauce. ♥

15

HUMMUS
Makes 2 cups

Tahini is ground sesame seeds and is available at health food stores. ♥ Serve this nutritious dip with fresh vegetables & warmed whole wheat pita bread. ♥ Try it for a light lunch. ♥

¼ c. plus 1 Tbsp. tahini

1 19 oz. can chick peas (garbanzo beans)

juice of one juicy lemon

2½ Tbsp. olive oil

2½ Tbsp. warm water

3 cloves garlic

½ tsp. salt

freshly ground pepper

Put everything in the food processor ~ whirl to blend thoroughly; scrape down sides of bowl as needed. Add more lemon juice if you think it needs it. ♥ It should be a thick dip. ♥

BAKED MONTRACHET
350° Serves Four

This should be served hot & is better for a small group rather than a large party. ♥

Put one petite Montrachet cheese log in a shallow bowl. Sprinkle on 1 Tbsp. basil or thyme leaves; pour over ½ c. olive oil ~ cover & marinate at room temperature overnight. Preheat oven to 350°. Combine ½ c. breadcrumbs, 1 tsp. basil or thyme & freshly ground pepper to taste. Roll the cheese in this mixture & bake 18~20 min. till lightly browned. Serve with Bremner Wafers. ♥ You can also slice the cheese, marinate it & roll each slice individually in breadcrumbs & serve them hot alongside a salad. ♥

OYSTERS ROCKEFELLER

450° Makes 1 dozen

I almost feel honored when someone makes these for me — they're that good! You couldn't ask for a more elegant beginning to a meal. ♥

1 doz. oysters, freshly shucked (loosen both top & bottom)
2 c. cooked spinach, finely chopped (fresh or frozen)
5 slices bacon, partially cooked, cut into 1 inch pieces
2 Tbsp. butter
1/4 c. onion, minced
1 clove garlic, minced
2 Tbsp. unbleached flour
1 1/4 c. heavy cream
3/4 c. Swiss cheese, grated
3/4 c. Muenster cheese, grated

Preheat oven to 450°. If frozen spinach is used, it must be thawed and well-drained. Cook the bacon till almost done but still soft; cut into 1" pieces. Put the butter in a skillet & sauté the onion & garlic until soft. Stir in flour & cook 1–2 min. Add cream, then spinach, & mix well. Remove from heat. Put a heaping Tbsp. of spinach mixture on each oyster; top with a piece of bacon. Combine the cheeses and put about 2 Tbsp. on each oyster. (At this point, the oysters can be covered & refrigerated till needed — up to two days.) Bake them, uncovered, in a shallow pan for about 15 min. till browned on top. Serve on a pretty tray with lemon wedges. ♥

CLAMS CASINO

450° Makes 1 dozen

Serve these with heated French bread for mopping up the garlic butter. ♥

1 doz. littleneck clams
4 Tbsp. garlic butter (recipe below)
4 Tbsp. red pepper, minced
4 slices bacon, partially cooked
3 Tbsp. bread crumbs
3 Tbsp. Parmesan cheese, grated

Preheat oven to 450°. Open clams; loosen meat from both top & bottom & pour off liquid. Make garlic butter. Cook bacon till almost done but still soft; cut into 1" pieces. On each clam, put a tsp. of garlic butter, a tsp. of red pepper, a piece of bacon, & cover with a mixture of bread crumbs & grated Parmesan. Bake on a cookie sheet for 10 min. till browned. Serve with lemon wedges. ♥

GARLIC BUTTER

Cream together: ½ c. butter, 2 cloves minced garlic, ¼ c. minced shallots, ¼ c. minced parsley, 2 Tbsp. lemon juice, & 2 Tbsp. white wine (opt.). ♥

♥ Helpful hint: Push cloves of garlic into ground near base of rose bushes & raspberries ~ helps to deter pests & improve growth. ♥

GUACAMOLE

Use only the bumpy, thick-skinned avocados. The smooth, thin-skinned ones are watery and have very little flavor. ♥

2 avocados, mashed
1 tbsp. grated onion
1 tbsp. fresh lemon juice

1 tsp. salt
1/4 tsp. chili powder
1 diced tomato

Mash avocados with potato masher. Add all other ingredients and mix well. Serve with tortilla chips or with Quesadillas. ♥

QUESADILLAS

Melt a pat of butter in a large skillet. Lay a flour tortilla in the pan and cover it with thinly sliced jack cheese. Put another tortilla on top of the cheese. Cover the pan and cook over low heat until cheese is almost melted. Flip the tortilla over and brown the other side. Cut it like a pie and serve with sour cream and/or salsa. ♥ I like to put chopped mild green chili peppers in with the cheese, or if you like it hot, try it with sliced jalapeño peppers. Yum. ♥

♥ ♥ ♥ ♥ ♥

"Many's the long night I've dreamed of cheese —
    toasted mostly."   ♥ Robert Louis Stevenson ♥

SUSHI

Makes 2 rolls & 6 rice cakes

Sushi is easy to make ~ in fact, after the first time you probably won't need a recipe. Also, I will give you just a couple of ideas for fillings, but you will see that your imagination is the only limit. The ingredients are avail~ able at health food stores and gourmet food shops. ♥

1 pkg. sushi nori (edible seaweed)
1 c. short grain white rice, uncooked
¼ c. rice vinegar
1 Tbsp. sugar
1 pkg. wasabi powder
1 pkg. pickled ginger
soy sauce
2 stalks celery
2 carrots
1 cucumber
6 large shrimp

Sushi platter suggestion ~ chives for stems ~ sushi for flowers. ♥

You'll also need long wooden picks & a "su", a bamboo sushi mat.

Cook the rice. Cut celery & carrots into thin strips. Peel, seed, & quarter the cucumber. Vegetables should be very fresh & crisp. In a tiny cup, mix 1 Tbsp. wasabi powder with just enough water to make a thick paste. Turn the cup upside-down on the counter to "set-up" (about 10 min.) Mix together the vinegar & the sugar. Stir the mixture into the cooked rice. Cool the rice slightly. Take one sheet of nori, lay it on top of the su with the rough side up. Put about ¾ c. rice mixture on ½ of the nori sheet, closest to you. Pack it firmly and evenly ~

When you roll it you won't want it to be too fat, so keep that in mind. Cut a ridge into the rice about ⅓ of the way up & lay in some thin strips of carrot & celery or cucumber, any combinations you like, but keep color in mind. Very gently, using su to begin, roll the nori away from you, tucking in the edge. Finish the roll with just your hands & use the su to round it out. Fill in the ends firmly with extra rice. With a very sharp knife slice the roll in ½" pieces, wiping the knife on a wet cloth between each cut. Serve with a little wasabi (very HOT) mixed with soy sauce to taste, & ginger on the side (discard dark blood root from pkg. of ginger). ♥ To make Rice Cakes: Wet hands & salt well so rice won't stick to them. Put a Tbsp. of rice into your palm & make a firm little oval cake ⬭ about 1½" long. Peel the shrimp, leaving the tail on. Take a wooden pick & push it through the shrimp all the way up, making it very straight & flat. (Shrimp curl when boiled & you want them to cook flat & then lie flat on top of the rice cake.) Do all the shrimp in this manner and drop them, picks & all, into boiling water ~ when water comes back to boil, they are done. Cool them, then butterfly them, & remove vein. Lay them over rice cakes. Cut a ¼" strip of nori off a sheet & wrap it around the rice cake & shrimp just once. Cut off the extra & wet your finger & touch the edges of the nori so it will hold ⬭. Serve with ginger & the wasabi ~ soy sauce mixture. ♥ If a roll should ever split, you can fix it with a little bit of moistened nori. ♥ A simple, clean presentation is the hallmark of Japanese cooking, so be creative when serving sushi. ♥ Ideas for sushi rolls : a lovely combination would be thin slices of avocado, crab meat, & cucumber. Another would be lobster meat, radish, & celery. Try your own ideas. ♥

Rice cake with radish sprouts ♥

GUACAMOLE SHRIMP BITES

Makes about 60

Festive tasty treats. ♥

30 med. shrimp	60 round tortilla chips
Guacamole (p.19)	1 bunch cilantro (garnish)

Shell & devein the shrimp; drop them into boiling water. Cook 2 min. (no more) ~ drain them & refresh them in cold water. Make the guacamole & keep both shrimp & guacamole refrigerated until ready to serve. When ready, spread each tortilla chip with guacamole; cut the shrimp in half & place one shrimp-half on each chip. Garnish each with one cilantro leaf & serve. ♥

SMOKED BLUEFISH PÂTÉ

Makes 1½ cups

Creamy delicious ~ serve with crackers or fill celery stalks. ♥

⅓ lb. smoked bluefish	5 drops Tabasco sauce
8 oz. cream cheese, softened	2 Tbsp. fresh dill, minced
1 Tbsp. Worcestershire sauce	2 Tbsp. parsley, minced

"Crumble" the bluefish. Whip the cream cheese well & stir in bluefish. Add all other ingredients & cream together. Refrigerate. ♥

22

CREAM CHEESE & PESTO MOLD

Makes about 6 cups

Buttery layers of cream cheese with pesto make a dramatic looking centerpiece at a party. ♥

1 lb. unsalted butter
2 8oz. pkg. cream cheese
Pesto (recipe p. 79)

¼ c. pine nuts
1 Tbsp. butter
1 sprig fresh basil

You'll need a piece of cheesecloth, 18" square, double thickness, for this recipe & an 8 cup mold (a clean flowerpot will do fine!). Make the pesto. Cream the butter & cheese together until smooth & well blended. Wet the cheesecloth & wring it dry. Line the mold as smoothly as possible & drape excess over sides. You can have as many layers as you like, but you should start with the cheese & also end with it. I like alot of layers so I do 6 layers of cheese & 5 of pesto ~ it's best to divide the cheese and the pesto ahead of time so the layers will be even. After the mold is filled, fold the excess cheesecloth over the top & press down firmly. Refrigerate for 2 hours, then invert onto serving dish & gently remove cheesecloth. (can be covered with plastic wrap & refrigerated for up to 5 days.) Before serving, melt 1 Tbsp. butter in small skillet & cook the pine nuts over medium heat till lightly browned; drain on paper towels; cool. Arrange the nuts in a circle around the top of cheese; place a sprig of fresh basil in the center & serve. ♥ Crackers, bread & raw vegies are good accompaniments. ♥ I like to pile the cheese on fresh French bread & top it with a thick slice of radish. ♥

STUFFED FRENCH BREAD

250°

I love how this looks at a Christmas party ~ a pretty, edible package. ♥ By changing the color of the ribbon, or by adding American flags, Valentines, or whatever, it would be darling at any celebration. ♥

2 8oz. pkg. cream cheese, softened
2 cans chopped clams, drained
2 Tbsp. lemon juice
½ c. chopped fresh parsley
2 round loaves of French bread

½ c. minced green onion
1 tsp. salt
1 Tbsp. Worcestershire sauce
½ tsp. hot pepper sauce

Mix ingredients ~ Cut off the top of one of the loaves of bread ~ hollow out the bottom part & fill it with the cream cheese mixture. Put the lid back on & wrap the loaf in foil. Bake at 250° for 3 hours. Cut the other loaf into dipping-sized pieces & serve alongside. For Christmas choose a wide plaid ribbon, set the lid off to the side a little, and hook the bow down with a straight pin ~ You'll want it to look like a Christmas present. ♥

NASTURTIUMS

Serves Six

This is a spectacular summer appetizer ~ a plateful of big, beautiful (edible) orange flowers stuffed with a sweetened cream cheese mixture ~ Delicious! ♥ They grow them year~round in a wonderful solar greenhouse here on the island ~ you can grow them outside in the summer (they also deter pests & improve growth & flavor in your vegetable garden) or look for them in health food stores or gourmet food shops. ♥

3/4 c. cream cheese
4 Tbsp. sour cream
1 Tbsp. fresh lemon juice
3 tsp. honey

1 tsp. vanilla
1/3 c. chopped walnuts
1/4 c. chopped raisins
18 nasturtiums & leaves

Soften cream cheese. Blend all ingredients well (except for flowers). Form into tiny balls & chill 1/2 hour. Fit a ball into the center of each flower. Arrange on a plate covered with the large dark green nasturtium leaves. ♥ For extra prettiness, top each filled nasturtium with a fresh Violet or a tiny Forget~me~not. Other edible flowers include: Day Lily, Johnny~jump~up, & Gladiolus. ♥ Be sure no pesticides are used on the flowers, O.K.?

"Things that haven't been done before,
Those are the things to try;
Columbus dreamed of an unknown shore
At the rim of the far~flung sky."
Edgar Guest ♥

WON TON

Makes about 60

Serve these with Chinese Dumplings (p.13) & some hot sake for a nice change. ♥

1 lb. ground pork
1 egg, beaten
1 tsp. sesame oil
2 Tbsp. soy sauce
1 clove garlic, minced

4 Tbsp. green onion, minced
2 tsp. cornstarch
1 lb. won ton wrappers
peanut oil for frying
Sweet & Sour Sauce

Thoroughly combine pork, egg, sesame oil, soy sauce, garlic, green onion & cornstarch. Won ton wrappers dry out quickly so lay a damp cloth on your counter top & fold it in half. Put 1 tsp. of filling in the center of each wrapper; moisten edges with water & fold into triangle shape; put under damp cloth. Repeat until all filling is used. Heat about 4" oil in large pan over med. high heat. Fry won ton, a few at a time, until browned on both sides. Drain on paper towels & keep warm in a 200° oven till all are done. Serve hot. ♥ These can be frozen. To reheat, do not defrost; place on cookie sheet & bake 15 min. at 350°. ♥

Sweet & Sour Sauce

2/3 c. brown sugar
2/3 c. rice wine vinegar
2/3 c. water
1/3 c. catsup

1½ Tbsp. soy sauce
2 tsp. Worcestershire sauce
2 tsp. ginger, minced
3 tsp. cornstarch

Combine sugar & vinegar in a saucepan & bring to boil. Reduce heat & simmer 5 min., stirring occasionally. Stir in all other ingredients & simmer 15 min. more. Serve hot with won ton. ♥

FLOWERS & CHEESE

They're guaranteed to be the prettiest things at the party. ♥ The flowers keep their vibrant colors & the cheeses shimmer in the wine glaze. They make a beau~ tiful house present. ♥

The last time I made these I used a petite Montrachet log, a wedge of Cheddar, a small wheel of Brie & a rectangular piece of jack. The different shapes & colors add texture but you definitely want to use cheese with an edible rind. For flowers (pesticide free) you can use nasturtiums, violets, roses, Johnny~jump-ups, lavender, chive flowers, honeysuckle or forget-me-nots— all edible. Sprigs & leaves of herbs are so delicate ─ use chives, rosemary, parsley, thyme & basil ─ just to name a few. Put the cold cheese on a wire rack in a shallow pan ~ arrange your flowers on top & then: Mix together 1 envelope plain gelatin & 2 cups good dry white wine in a saucepan & set aside for about 5 minutes. Cook over medium heat, stirring, till gelatin is dissolved & mixture is clear. Cool quickly by pouring into another bowl & setting it into a larger bowl of ice & water. Stir gently occasionally until mixture becomes syrupy. Remove flowers from cheese; spoon over your 1st coat of cooled gelatin; let it get a little tacky; lay on flowers the way you like them. Refrigerate 20 min., and spoon on another coat of gelatin. Again refrigerate & continue this way with a couple more coats ─ do sides & top & cover flowers completely. ♥ Gelatin can be reheated if it should become too thick. Cheeses can be made a day ahead & kept covered (invert a bowl over them) in your refrigerator till ready to serve. ♥ Simply beautiful !

27

"April in New England
is like first love."
Gladys Tabor

TRADITION

A lovely word that brings up childhood memories and feelings of security. With families going their own ways so much these days, some of the old traditions have been put aside and maybe even forgotten. But that doesn't mean you can't start new ones, better ones and even happier ones. The mother of one of my friends gives her a nightgown every Christmas 🎄. When she mentioned this she said it with kind of an embarrassed roll of the eyes ~ but it was obvious that the continuity of this tradition pleased her. She depends on that nightgown! 🔔 At our house we had the same menu every single Thanksgiving, and now to substitute or change anything for me would be doing major damage to Thanks~ giving! 🦃 Here are some other ideas for traditions, and I'm sure you can think of lots more:

- ♥ Have a guest book in your house ~ Ask for names and "Words of Wisdom, Quotes, etc." ~ a wonderful way to re~ member your friends and family on special occasions.
- ♥ Tie bells on the bread basket with a narrow ribbon ~ passing the bread makes a nice happy Christmas sound.
- ♥ Chop down your own Christmas tree ~ make it a party with hot cider and popcorn.
- ♥ Easter egg hunt ~ Easter egg coloring party (p.111)
- ♥ Sunday dinners at four o'clock
- ♥ Sunday rides in the country
- ♥ Mom cooks your favorite on your birthday.
- ♥ Root beer floats made with homemade ice cream every 4th of July

FOR YOUR GUESTS

- ♥ Clean fresh sheets and blankets on the bed.
- ♥ Flowers ~ one rose, a tiny bouquet of wildflowers..
- ♥ Make up a big plate of sandwiches, like roast beef with dilled Havarti cheese, sweet pickle, thinly sliced red onion and lettuce ~ good sandwiches! They'll be there all weekend when anyone is hungry & you can put them in a Styrofoam cooler with other goodies for the trip home.
- ♥ Have small picture books, magazines, quick reads.
- ♥ Plan things: a picnic, a concert, a hike in the woods.
- ♥ Put grapes and nuts in their room, and a container of fresh water with a glass.
- ♥ Have a fluffy covered hot water bottle.
- ♥ In the winter, summer herbs for good smells.
- ♥ Big Idea: My house is very tiny and I wanted a place for my guests to feel comfortable, so out in the backyard I built a little "shed" exactly the size of two king beds ~ ½ of it is bed, and the other half is chairs, a table, etc. It's whitewashed ~ dried flowers hang from the rafters ~ no electricity, but lots of candles & windows. Very cozy & romantic. ♥

SOUPS

"It breathes reassurance, it offers consolation;
after a weary day it promotes sociability . . . .
There is nothing like a bowl of hot soup. . . . "
~ The Soup Book, Louis DeGouy ~

CHICKEN STOCK

In comparison to rich homemade chicken stock, the canned stuff is like brown salted water! It's very easy to make ~ and you'll love having the cooked chicken meat around for munching. ♥

1 lg. or 2 small chickens
hearts & gizzards from chicken
2 Tbsp. butter
1 Tbsp. oil
3 carrots, chopped
3 ribs of celery with leaves, chopped

1 lg. onion, chopped
2 bay leaves
1 bunch parsley
8 peppercorns
water to cover

Everything can be very roughly chopped & unpeeled as it will be cooked for hours & then strained out of the soup ~ all you want are the flavors & the vitamins. ♥ Melt the butter & oil in a deep soup pot ~ put in the chopped hearts & gizzards & fry over med. high heat. When well browned, add ½ c. water to pot & scrape brown bits off bottom ~ add all remaining ingredients. Leave chickens whole, or cut in half only. Fill pot with water just to cover. Bring to boil, then reduce heat to simmer & cook till chicken is done ~ about 1 hr. Remove chicken from pot; cool to touch. Remove all meat to your refrigerator & put the skin & bones back into the soup pot. Leave the pot simmering, with lid slightly askew, for about 3 hours or more ~ it doesn't really matter ~ but don't allow water level to get too low ~ add more when needed. When you're ready, strain the soup; discard the vegies & bones ~ put the broth in the refrigerator, uncovered, overnight. The fat will rise to the top, harden, & you can just scrape it right off. Beneath, you'll have a beautiful rich broth all ready to use for French Onion Soup (p. 34) & lots of others. ♥ If you want it for sauce or gravy, boil down till very strong; pour into ice cube trays; freeze; remove to plastic bags; use as needed. ♥

CHICKEN BARLEY SOUP

Makes 8~10 servings ♥

Truly the magical elixir ~ the well-known cure for the common cold ♥.

Chicken Stock (p.32)   3 stalks celery, sliced
2 Tbsp. butter   1 c. parsley, minced
1 lg. onion, chopped   salt & pepper, to taste
2 c. barley, rinsed   chicken meat, chopped
3 carrots, sliced   Parmesan cheese (opt.)

Reheat the stock; taste for strength ~ if not strong enough, boil down till taste is correct. Melt butter in skillet; add onion & slow~cook till soft & golden. Rinse barley & pick over for rocks. When stock is boiling, add barley & simmer till the barley is almost cooked through & soft. Add slow~cooked onions, carrots, celery, & parsley. Cook until carrots are just tender. (Don't overcook the vegies!) Add salt & pepper & chopped chicken ~ Heat through and serve. Try a little Parmesan sprinkled on each serving. ♥ The amounts of vegetables & chicken can be altered, depending on how much broth you have. ♥ From a large chicken, I usually get about 8 cups of stock. ♥ If you'd rather have chicken ~ potato soup, substitute diced potatoes for barley & add them at the same time as other vegetables. ♥ Sometimes, for a change of flavor, I add thyme to the soup. ♥ Experiment. ♥!

33

FRENCH ONION
SOUP

Serves Six ♥

A hearty, classic soup. It's the long, slow cooking of the onions that brings out the mellow, rich flavor. ♥ Have it with a Caesar Salad (p. 52) for a nice cozy dinner ~ and baked bananas (p. 147) for dessert. ♥

5 c. onions, thinly sliced
4 Tbsp. butter
1 clove garlic, minced
3 Tbsp. flour
8 c. rich chicken stock (p. 32)

1 tsp thyme leaves
1 tsp. Dijon mustard
freshly ground pepper
French bread croutons (below)
1 lb. Swiss or Gruyère cheese

Put the onions & butter in a large, heavy soup pan. Stir to coat with butter. Cover pan & cook very slowly for about 15 min., stirring once or twice. Uncover & cook for another half hour, stirring often until onions are golden brown ~ very slow cooking. Stir in garlic; cook 2~3 min. Add flour; stir & cook 2~3 min. more. Add stock, thyme, mustard & pepper (to taste). Bring to boil ~ lower heat & simmer 30~40 min. Put soup in oven-proof bowls. To each bowl add 2~3 French bread croutons ~ allow them to expand ~ they form the base for cheese to sit upon. Add about ½ c. grated cheese on top of each bowl. Bake in 425° oven for 30 min. till cheese is golden brown. ♥

Croutons

Cut rounds of French bread about 3/4" thick. Place in 325° oven for 15 min. to dry. Brush both sides with olive oil ~ rub with cut garlic clove. Bake another 10~15 min. till lightly browned. ♥

♥ ♥ ♥

BEAN SOUP

Serves Six

In late Fall, when the first chill comes, this is my
first and favorite soup to make. It makes my house
smell good as it slowly bubbles away the afternoon.
This is the kind of soup that sticks to your ribs,
and it's good for you too. ♥

1½ lbs. smoked ham hocks   2 medium onions, chopped
1 lb. pkg. small white beans   2 bay leaves
3 sliced carrots   salt and pepper to taste
3 stalks celery sliced   water to cover

Put all ingredients in a soup pot. Bring to boil. Reduce
heat and simmer partially covered for 3~4 hours. It
will get very thick, so add water when you think it
needs it. Somewhere down the line remove the ham
hocks from the soup, and cool them. Cut the meat off
the bones, discard the fat and return the meat and
bones to the pot. When you're ready to serve, remove
the bones and bay leaves & bring out some crusty
bread and butter. ♥

TOMATO SOUP

Makes 4 cups

Make this in the summer when the tomatoes are the sweetest — it's clear, light, and elegant. Freeze some so you can enjoy the taste of summer all winter long. ♥

2½ lbs. fresh ripe tomatoes   1 green pepper, chopped
2 carrots, sliced   3 whole cloves
3 stalks celery, chopped   2 Tbsp. lemon juice
1 onion, chopped   salt and pepper

Coarsely chop the tomatoes and put them in a soup pot with 1 cup water. Add carrots, celery, onion, green pepper, and cloves. Bring to a boil, reduce heat, and simmer for 20 minutes. Strain. Add lemon juice and salt and pepper to taste. Very few delicious calories. ♥

KALE SOUP

Serves Eight

Full of good healthy things & somewhat of a tradition here on the island. ♥ Serve it with Best Biscuits, p.140. ♥

1 lb. kale, thoroughly washed
1 lb. linguica (or, sweet Italian sausage)
3 Tbsp. butter
2 Tbsp. olive oil
½ c. celery, chopped
1 c. onions, chopped
½ c. carrots, chopped
2 cloves garlic, minced

4 med. potatoes, diced
8 c. Chicken Stock, p.32
2 c. canned beef broth
2 lbs. tomatoes, fresh or canned
1 19oz. can garbanzo beans
1 tsp. basil
1 tsp. thyme
salt, fresh pepper, to taste

Use tender part of kale only — leaves only, no stems. Chop into fairly small pieces — set aside. If using fresh tomatoes, peel, seed & chop them and set aside. Prick linguica with fork & drop into boiling water for 10 min., to get rid of the fat. Cut into ½" slices & quarter them. (If using Italian sausage, fry it; drain fat; reserve.) Melt the butter & oil in a large heavy soup pot; add celery, onions, carrots & garlic. Cook slowly till soft — add potatoes, chicken stock & beef broth. Bring to boil; reduce to simmer and cook, partially covered, for 15 min., till potatoes are cooked through. Stir in tomatoes & garbanzo beans. Simmer 15 min. more. Add kale, linguica (or sausage), basil, thyme and salt & pepper to taste. Simmer about 7 min. more — Serve. ♥

♥ ♥ ♥

"Chance is perhaps the pseudonym of God when He did not want to sign." Anatole France ♥

VICHYSSOISE

Serves Four

I have tasted many variations on this soup but this one has it all: creamy texture and delicate flavor. It can set the tone for an elegant dinner. ♥

1¼ lbs. leeks
1 small onion, chopped
¼ c. butter
1¾ lbs. potatoes, peeled and quartered
1 qt. chicken broth
1 Tbsp. fresh chives
1 tsp. dried chervil
1 tsp. salt
¼ tsp. white pepper
1 c. whipping cream
1 c. whole milk

Chop the white part only of leeks. Sauté the leeks and onion in melted butter in a 3-qt. saucepan over medium heat until onion is tender, about 10 min. Stir in potatoes and chicken broth. Heat to boiling ~ reduce heat ~ simmer uncovered for 45 min. Remove from heat ~ Cool slightly. Put half the potato mixture in blender & blend at high speed until puréed. Transfer to large bowl and repeat with remaining potato mixture. Stir in remaining ingredients, cover and chill well. ♥

GAZPACHO

This is the freshest Gazpacho I've ever tasted ~ I think it's because it's not cooked. When I want to serve it as a main course, I add three cooked (boiled) cold prawns to each serving. It makes a fabulous Summer repast. ♥

In your blender:
10 oz. cold tomato juice
½ med. cucumber, cut up
1 med. tomato, cut up
1 tbsp. sugar
¼ c. red wine vinegar
¼ c. salad oil

To blended ingredients, add:
2½ c. tomato juice
1 med. tomato, chopped
½ med. cucumber, chopped
1 small onion, finely chopped
2 celery stalks, diced
2 green onions, green part only, chopped
½ zucchini, chopped
1 small green pepper, finely chopped

(Add or subtract any vegetables you like; make the pieces big enough to chew on, but not so big that they don't fit together on a spoon.) Serve very cold ~ make your own croutons (p. 52), add a big dollop of sour cream to each serving ~ and don't forget the shrimp. ♥ Of course, the croutons, sour cream & shrimp will up the calorie-count ~ so use those only for Special Occasions, or when you've a mind to. ♥

CIOPPINO

Serves 8~10

This special soup should be served in very wide~mouthed, shallow bowls ~ it is almost like a stew. It's also lots of fun to eat and has a thin delicious broth. ♥

3/4 c. butter
2 medium onions, chopped
2 garlic cloves, minced
1 large bunch fresh parsley, finely chopped
2 cans (1 lb. 12 oz.) whole tomatoes
2 cans (14 oz.) chicken broth
2 bay leaves
1 Tbsp. basil
½ tsp. each : thyme and oregano
1 c. water
1½ c. dry white wine
1½ lbs. extra large shrimp
1½ lbs. scallops (small "Bay" are sweetest)
1½ dozen fresh small clams
1½ dozen fresh mussels
1½ c. crabmeat chunks
Any other firm whitefish you'd like

Melt butter in a large kettle, add onions, garlic and parsley ~ cook slowly until onion is soft. Add tomatoes (breaking into chunks) with the liquid, broth, bay leaves, basil, thyme, oregano, water and wine. Cover and simmer 30 min. Add all fish, and bring to a boil. Cover and simmer 5~7 min., till the clams are open. Serve hot with a Spinach Salad (p. 53) and french bread. ♥

SCALLOP VEGETABLE SOUP

Serves One

Make this for yourself — then double it & make it for someone you love ♥. It's spicy, colorful & delicious — not to
mention healthy! Good with Beer Bread Muffins (p.151).

1½ Tbsp. butter
1 shallot, minced
1 sm. clove garlic, minced
1 Tbsp. fresh dill, minced
2 Tbsp. parsley, minced
1½ Tbsp. fresh lemon juice
⅓ c. white wine

6 asparagus tops
6 mushrooms, sliced
1 rib celery, sliced
1 tomato, chopped
¼ lb. bay scallops
freshly ground pepper

Melt butter in large skillet. Add shallot, garlic, dill,
parsley, lemon juice & wine. Cook over low heat till shallot
is tender. Add asparagus, mushrooms, celery & tomato.
Cover & cook till tomato begins to release juices — stir
occasionally. Add scallops & pepper to taste. Stir &
cook, covered, over medium heat, for about 4 min. till
scallops are opaque. Don't overcook scallops. Serve ♥.

"Be not forgetful to entertain strangers: For
thereby some have entertained angels unawares."
New Testament

BUTTERNUT BISQUE

Serves Six

Rich orange color ~ thickened with potato rather than cream ~ very nutritious & low ~ calorie. ♥

2 ~ 2½ lb. Butternut squash
2 Tbsp. butter
2 carrots, sliced
1 onion, chopped
1 stalk celery, chopped

2 potatoes, peeled & cubed
5 ~ 6 c. chicken stock (canned is OK)
1½ tsp. curry powder
pinch each: nutmeg & ginger
sour cream for garnish (opt.)

My market peels & seeds their squash, which is very handy as it must be done for this soup. Cube it & set aside. Melt the butter in a lg. soup pot; add the carrots, onion & celery; sauté until soft. Stir the squash & potatoes into the vegetables. Add the stock; bring to boil, reduce heat & simmer, partially covered for 40 min. Add curry, nutmeg & ginger. Purée the soup in batches in a blender. Return to saucepan; add more stock if necessary to thin; salt & pepper to taste. Serve hot with a dollop of sour cream if you like. ♥

" By December the valley people are really dug in for winter. Wood is piled high in sheds, cabbages and pots are binned in the cellars, and squash and apples are stored." ♥

Gladys Tabor ♥

42

CREAM OF CAULIFLOWER
Serves Four

Good hot or cold — very quick to make. ♥

2 c. leeks, chopped	4 c. chicken broth
2 Tbsp. butter	1 c. heavy cream
2 Tbsp. oil	½ tsp. white pepper
1 large head cauliflower (4 c.)	2 Tbsp. snipped chives

Sauté leeks in butter & oil till soft & golden. Add cauliflower & chicken broth; bring to boil; reduce to simmer & cook until cauliflower is soft. Purée mixture in blender or food processor. Return to pan; add cream & pepper; reheat slowly (don't boil). Before serving, sprinkle with snipped chives. ♥

"The night shall be filled with music
And the cares that infest the day
Shall fold their tents like the Arabs,
And as silently steal away."
♥ Henry Wadsworth Longfellow

FISH CHOWDER

Serves Eight

Serve with a big basket of Cornmeal Muffins (p.142). ♥

2½~3 lb. whole cod fish	3 lg. potatoes, diced
2 pt. oysters, shucked	2 med. onions, chopped
2 pt. clams, shucked	1 potato, grated
2 ribs celery, chopped	1 pt. half & half
1 small onion, chopped	½ c. heavy cream
¼ c. parsley, chopped	3 Tbsp. butter
6 thick slices bacon	salt & pepper, to taste

Select a whole fish; ask the fish man to clean & filet it & chop the carcass to fit into soup pot. Reserve filets; put the carcass, the liquid from the oysters and clams, the celery, onion & parsley into a pot. Barely cover with water. Bring to boil & simmer, un- covered, until liquid boils down to about 2 cups. Meanwhile, cook the bacon crisp~remove from fat; reserve. Cook the potatoes in the bacon fat till tender; add onions, cook through & remove from heat. Strain the fish broth; return broth to pot & add grated potato. Simmer for 10 min; add potato onion mixture, oysters, clams & cod fish (cut into 1½" pieces). Cook gently 5 min. Stir in half & half, cream, butter, crumbled bacon, & salt & pepper to taste. (Thin with milk if necessary.) Heat through, but don't boil. Remove from heat; allow the soup to sit 1 hr. Reheat & serve. ♥

"I must go down to the seas again, to the lonely sea and the sky,
And all I ask is a tall ship and a star to steer her by ..." J. Masefield

ZUCCHINI SOUP

Serves Four

This tasty light soup resolves the problem of what to do with all those giant zucchinis your "friends" leave on your porch!

4 c. sliced zucchini
1 med. onion, chopped
3 Tbsp. butter
1 c. water
1 10 oz. can cream of chicken soup
1 c. milk
1 c. half & half
1 tsp. dried basil
salt and pepper

Sauté onion in butter several minutes. Add zucchini and water ~ Simmer 30 min. Remove from heat; cool slightly. Blend in blender at high speed until puréed. Return to saucepan. Add the rest of the ingredients and heat to simmering. Serve. ♥

"Hitch your wagon to a star."
Emerson ♥

45

"'Tis merry, merry in the spring,
And merry in the summer time,
And merry when the great winds sing
Through autumn's woodlands brown—
And in the winter, wild and cold,
'Tis merry, merry too."

William Howitt

SALAD DRESSINGS

Cheese and Herb

Makes 1¼ cups

1 c. mayonnaise

2 Tbsp. fresh lemon juice

⅓ c. grated Parmesan cheese

½ c. minced parsley

1 tsp. dried tarragon

1 clove minced garlic (opt.)

Mix well, cover & refrigerate. ♥

Cucumber Dill

Makes 2 cups

1⅓ c. peeled, seeded, chopped cucumber

2 Tbsp. minced red onion

2 Tbsp. minced parsley

1¼ c. mayonnaise

1 Tbsp. fresh lemon juice

1½ Tbsp. milk

1 tsp. dill weed

Mix well, cover & refrigerate ♥

Cream

Makes ½ cup

⅓ c. heavy cream

3 tsp. fresh lemon juice

½ tsp. white pepper

¼ tsp. salt

1 Tbsp. olive oil

1 Tbsp. peanut oil

Beat first four ingredients with whisk till foamy and creamy. Beat in oil slowly. Especially good on tender greens such as Boston or Bibb lettuce. ♥

Poppy Seed

Makes 1½ cups

1 egg yolk
1 tsp. Dijon mustard
3 Tbsp. honey
¼ c. lemon juice

1 tsp. paprika
fresh pepper to taste
1 c. oil
1½ Tbsp. poppy seeds

Put all ingredients except oil & poppy seeds into food processor & blend well. Slowly add oil until thickened. Stir in poppy seeds; cover & refrigerate. ♥

Cottage Cheese

Makes 1½ cups

1 c. cottage cheese
¼ c. buttermilk
1 tsp. dill weed
1 Tbsp. parsley, minced

½ tsp. celery seed
fresh pepper to taste
½ green pepper, minced
2 Tbsp. bleu cheese

Put the cottage cheese & buttermilk into blender — Blend well; pour into container Add all other ingredients & mix well. Cover & refrigerate. ♥

Diet

Makes 2½ cups

¼ c. apple juice
¼ c. fresh lemon juice
1 c. vegetable juice
⅓ c. green onion, minced

1 clove garlic, minced
⅓ c. celery, chopped
¼ c. parsley, minced
fresh pepper to taste

Blend all in blender; cover & refrigerate. ♥

MAYONNAISE

Makes 2 cups

With a food processor, it takes about 5 minutes to make your own mayonnaise and you won't believe the difference. ♥ Use it as is. For a special chicken salad, add a little curry & chutney to taste. ♥

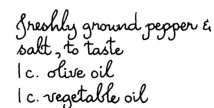

1 whole egg
2 egg yolks
3 Tbsp. fresh lemon juice
1 Tbsp. Dijon mustard

Freshly ground pepper & salt, to taste
1 c. olive oil
1 c. vegetable oil

Put the egg, yolks, lemon juice, mustard, pepper & salt into food processor and blend 1 minute. Blend the olive & vegetable oils together; then, with machine running, pour in the oil in a very slow, steady stream. That's it! Feel free to add any herbs you like to make flavored mayonnaise. ♥

TARTAR SAUCE

Makes 1 cup

Best made with homemade mayonnaise ~ delicious with fish. ♥

1 c. mayonnaise
1 Tbsp. capers
1 Tbsp. minced parsley

2 tsp. minced green onion
2 tsp. minced sweet pickle
1½ Tbsp. cider vinegar

Blend all ingredients & refrigerate. ♥

CHICKEN SALAD

Serves Six

I bake up chickens all the time just so I always have "leftovers". ♡ This healthy salad is one reason why. ♡

2 c. cooked cubed chicken   ½ c. cubed Cheddar cheese
2 ribs celery, chopped   3 minced green onions
1 green apple, cored & chopped   ⅓ c. mayonnaise mixed
½ c. chopped walnuts   with juice from ½ lemon

Mix all ingredients and serve on a bed of crisp lettuce leaves, torn in bite-sized pieces. ♡

EDIBLE SALAD BOWLS

These make adorable little salad bowls. You'll need a pkg. of egg roll skins (about 7" x 7") and 3 inches of hot oil (at about 375°). Lay egg roll skin flat on surface of oil ~ submerge, pressing with ladle to form bowls. When brown & crisp, drain upside-down on paper towels. Cool; fill with salad and serve. ♡

CAESAR SALAD

Serves Six

Lots of people turn their noses up to anchovies, so either mash them up very well, or use a food processor. They'll never know, and the anchovies add a delicious tang to the salad. ♥

1 lg. head romaine lettuce
½ c. olive oil
¼ c. fresh lemon juice
1 Tbsp. Dijon mustard
1 2oz. can anchovies

1 lg. egg
½ tsp. freshly ground
    pepper
⅓ c. grated Parmesan
2 c. homemade croutons

Wash lettuce early in the day so it has time to dry completely. Put the oil, lemon juice, mustard, anchovies, and egg into food processor and process for just a few seconds. Tear romaine into bite-sized pieces and put in salad bowl. Pour mixture over lettuce, sprinkle on pepper, Parmesan, and croutons. Toss the salad lightly and serve. ♥

HOMEMADE CROUTONS

Melt 2 parts butter to 1 part olive oil in a large skillet over medium high heat. Add 1 minced garlic clove. Cut French bread into ½" cubes. Don't overcrowd the skillet. Toss often to avoid burning. Toast well on all sides. ♥ These keep well in an airtight container. Delicious for salads and soups. ♥

SPINACH SALAD

Serves Six

I don't like bacon grease on my spinach salad! So I made up this slightly sweet dressing that seems to compliment the spinach just right. ♥

1 bunch spinach
½ c. cider vinegar
⅓ c. salad oil
¼ c. brown sugar

Freshly ground pepper &
Salt, to taste
4 hard-boiled egg whites
6 slices bacon, fried

Wash spinach very thoroughly and dry. Hard-boil eggs; fry the bacon till crispy, cool. Chop white parts of eggs only and reserve. (Save yolks for an egg salad.) In a shaker jar, mix vinegar, oil, brown sugar, salt & pepper. Shake well. Pour over spinach torn in bite-sized pieces. Toss lightly. Sprinkle on eggwhites and crumbled bacon. Serve. ♥

"'It's broccoli, dear.'
'I say it's spinach, and
I say the hell with it.'"
E.B. White ♥

STUFFED ARTICHOKES

Serves Six

A hearty first course, or a delicious light lunch served with creamy, crispy Fried Brie (p. 14). ♥

6 large artichokes
6 extra-large shrimp, peeled & cleaned
1 c. crab-meat
1 large tomato, diced
3/4 c. mayonnaise
curry powder, to taste
squeeze of lemon; paprika for color

Wash & trim artichokes; boil in salted water till stem is tender when pierced with fork. Cool and refrigerate. Drop shrimp into boiling water ~ when it comes back to boil, simmer for 1 min.; drain & refresh in cold water. Chill. When ready to serve, remove artichokes from the refrigerator, lightly spread leaves apart with your fingers & pull out the "choke," the tiny center leaves, making a cavity for filling. Scrape the bottom of cavity with spoon to remove "feathers." Mix mayonnaise with curry powder to taste. Chop shrimp & combine with crab-meat, tomato, and just enough curried mayonnaise to bind. Fill the arti~ chokes, squeeze lemon juice over all & sprinkle lightly with paprika. Serve with remaining mayonnaise for dipping. ♥

GREEN BEAN SALAD
Serves Four

One more good reason to have a garden! Fresh green beans with garlic, red pepper & dill ~ very pretty, very good. ♥

1 lb. fresh green beans
3 Tbsp. olive oil
3 Tbsp. fresh lemon juice
2 cloves garlic, minced
1 shallot, minced

2 Tbsp. red pepper, minced
1 Tbsp. dill, minced
1/8 tsp. dry mustard
1/4 tsp. salt
1/8 tsp. freshly ground pepper

Wash & trim ends of green beans but leave them whole. Cook the beans in boiling water for about 5 min. (they should still be crisp). Refresh immediately in cold water; set aside. Combine all remaining ingredients & mix well. Pour over beans & refrigerate 1 hour before serving. Serve cool, but not cold. ♥

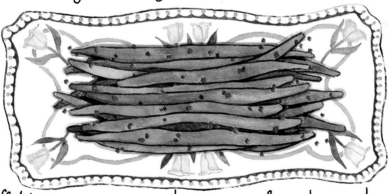

"Happiness grows at our own firesides, and
is not to be picked in strangers' gardens."
Douglas Jerrold ♥

55

SHRIMP SALAD

A refreshing combination of flavors — very bright. ♥
  Large cooked shrimp, chopped
  Avocado (thick & bumpy skinned)
  Fresh pink grapefruit sections
  Mayonnaise
  Orange juice
Put an equal amount of chopped shrimp, cubed avocado & pink grapefruit sections into a bowl. Dress with a little mayonnaise sweetened & thinned with orange juice. Serve chilled. ♥

CRAB SALAD

You can serve this on toasted English muffins, on top of a chilled avocado half or on a bed of crisp lettuce. ♥
  2 c. fresh or frozen crab meat
  1/3. c mayonnaise
  2 Tbsp. fresh lemon juice
  3 green onions, minced
  2 stalks celery, finely chopped
  2 tsp. celery seed
Chop the crab meat & combine with all other ingredients. Chill before serving. ♥

SUMMER SALAD

The fresher the ingredients the better ~ homegrown tomatoes
& basil, balsamic vinegar & the finest olive oil ~ truly a summer
delight. ♥

Fresh basil, leaves only
Fresh tomatoes, sliced
Buffalo Mozzarella cheese, sliced
olive oil
balsamic vinegar
Freshly ground pepper
salt

Arrange the basil, tomatoes & cheese on a platter ~ the point
is to eat a bite of all three together so a little layering is in
order. Drizzle a bit of oil & vinegar over all; sprinkle on
freshly ground pepper & salt to taste. Serve chilled. ♥

"August for the people and their favourite
    islands. Daily the steamers sidle up to
meet the effusive welcome of the pier."
        ♥ W. H. Auden ♥

CEVICHE

Serves Four as Salad

Fifteen years ago I went to Mexico City quite often, where I discovered Ceviche. I loved it ~ in fact, I would get off the plane and go directly to the restaurant in the airport for my Ceviche "fix" ~ I can still eat it by the gallon! The secret is to use fish that is practically still alive ~ it has to be fresh. The juice from the limes "cooks" the fish, and along with the fresh vegetables, you can't find a dish much healthier or better tasting. ♥

1 lb. fresh bay scallops	½ green pepper, minced
juice from 8 limes	½ c. parsley, minced
2 tomatoes, finely chopped	freshly ground pepper
5 green onions with tops, minced	1½ Tbsp. finest olive oil
2 ribs of celery, thinly sliced	⅛ c. fresh cilantro, minced (opt)

Rinse the scallops and put them in a bowl with lime juice to cover. Chill all day or overnight until the scallops are opaque. After that, pour off about half of the juice and add the remaining ingredients. Mix well and serve chilled. ♥ Feel free to experiment with this ~ if you like more or less of some vegetables, add or sub-tract. Cilantro is a wonderful herb used in many Mexican dishes ~ it looks like parsley ~ and I know it's unavailable in some places. So, it's optional, but it does add the authentic flavor. Also, if you can't get bay scallops, you can use a pound of any very fresh boned white fish, such as halibut, red snapper, flounder, or swordfish. ♥ Make up a bowl of this and keep it around for summer munching. ♥

FRUIT COMPOTE

350° Serves Six

Absolutely delicious. ♥ Use unsweetened fruit for this. It would be great with ham, Cornish Game Hens (p.104), or Veal Birds (p.97). Pour over heavy cream and you can also serve it for dessert. ♥

1 can pineapple slices
1 can peach halves
1 can apricots
1 can pear halves

½ c. apricot juice
4 Tbsp. butter, melted
½ c. brown sugar
½ c. coarsely chopped walnuts

Preheat oven to 350°. Drain fruit well ~ reserve apricot juice. Arrange dry fruit in baking dish. Cover with mixture of apricot juice (½ c.), melted butter & brown sugar. Sprinkle on walnuts; bake for 30 minutes till bubbly. Serve hot. ♥

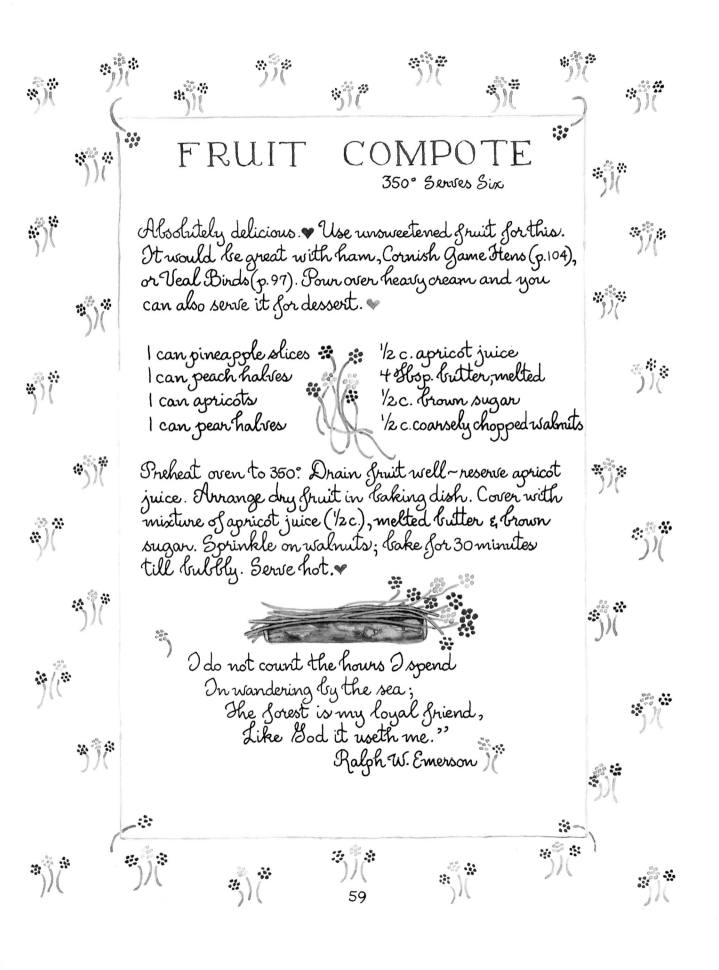

I do not count the hours I spend
In wandering by the sea;
The forest is my loyal friend,
Like God it useth me."
Ralph W. Emerson

59

PASTA SALAD

Serves Fifteen (or more)

A great big colorful salad that's perfect for large crowds ~ barbecues & picnics 🇺🇸 Also, good just to have around to appease the munchies. ♥

1 lb. corkscrew pasta
½ lb. tortellini with cheese
½ c. plus 1 Tbsp. olive oil
6 cloves garlic, minced
1 bunch broccoli, in small flowerettes
2 med. zucchini, sliced & quartered
1½ c. snow peas (or 2 pkg. frozen)

2 sweet red peppers, chopped
1 green pepper, chopped
1 6 oz. can pitted black olives
4 tomatoes, chopped
1 c. Parmesan cheese, grated
½ c. Romano cheese, grated
Freshly ground pepper

Cook the pasta according to package instructions. Drain & put into a large bowl. Pour oil into saucepan; add garlic & cook slowly till garlic is light brown. Set aside to cool. Lightly blanch broccoli, zucchini, and snow peas ~ refresh in cold water & set aside. Toss the pasta with garlic oil ~ add rest of ingredients & toss very gently. Serve ♥ Two things of importance : don't let garlic get dark-colored while cooking in oil AND don't overcook blanched vegies ~ they should be firm in shape, but tender to the bite. ♥ Best served at room temperature. ♥ "America! America!

JULY 4TH PICNIC   God shed His grace on thee." ♥ K. Bates

POTATO SALAD

Serves Eight

The fans go crazy for this delicious and different potato salad. Have it for a picnic or a barbecue. ♥

2 lbs. red potatoes, scrubbed & halved
½ lb. bacon, chopped
½ c. shallots, finely chopped
¼ c. olive oil
½ c. red wine vinegar
1 c. parsley, finely chopped
½ c. red onion, chopped
½ c. celery, chopped
salt & freshly ground pepper

Boil potatoes till fork~tender, drain them, cut them into bite-sized pieces, and put them in a large bowl. Fry the bacon crisp and reserve. Pour out all but about 3 Tbsp. of the bacon fat & sauté the shallots in the fat very slowly, till soft. Pour the shallots & the bacon fat over the hot potatoes; add the oil, vinegar, parsley, onion, celery, and crumbled bacon. Toss very gently, but thoroughly. Salt & pepper to taste. Serve at room temperature. Cover & refrigerate leftovers. ♥

"Good Americans, when they die, go to Paris."
Thomas Appleton ♥

RAINBOW JELL-O

I'm not a big Jell-O fan, but this one is so gorgeous and so festive looking—you'll have to try it for a holiday dinner. The kids love it and the cold, smooth texture is a nice contrast in a heavy holiday meal. ♥

1 6 oz. pkg. orange Jell-O
1 6 oz. pkg. lemon Jell-O
1 6 oz. pkg. lime Jell-O
1 6 oz. pkg. cherry Jell-O
4 c. (2 pints) sour cream

Dissolve the orange Jell-O in 2 c. boiling water. To 1/2 c. of the liquefied Jell-O, add 1 c. sour cream and stir well. Pour sour cream/Jell-O mixture into a 9×13 glass baking dish and reserve remaining 1 1/2 c. orange Jell-O. Put the baking dish on a level shelf of your refrigerator and chill until set. When firm, pour reserved orange Jell-O over creamy layer; chill until firm. Repeat with remaining colors of Jell-O— each with a creamy layer and a clear layer. ♥

"Glory be to God for dappled things."
♥ Gerard M. Hopkins ♥

62

TABBOULI

Serves Six

Delicious, nutritious and highly addictive!
Serve it on a bed of crisp lettuce. ♥

1 c. bulgar wheat
5 green onions, minced
2 tomatoes, diced
½ c. parsley, minced
3 Tbsp. fresh mint, minced
1 lg. carrot, grated
5 Tbsp. olive oil
⅓ c. fresh lemon juice
Freshly ground pepper, to taste

Put the bulgar in a bowl with cold water to cover. Let
stand for 1 hour to soften. Drain well & squeeze
dry in a towel. Toss in a bowl with all
other ingredients. Chill well to blend
flavors. ♥

63

BEAN SALAD
Serves Fifteen or more

This is a delicious munchable salad. ♥ If you're avoiding animal protein you can add rice to this dish making a complete vegetable protein. ♥

4 c. dried beans (see below) ♥
1 c. green beans
1 red onion, finely chopped
1 red pepper, diced
4 Tbsp. parsley, chopped
freshly ground pepper, to taste
Vinaigrette (see below)

♥Use 1 cup each of different dried beans — make color be part of the criterion — choose from pinto beans, kidney beans, white beans, lentils, lima beans or garbanzo beans. Wash & pick over beans for rocks. Cook each kind of bean (including green beans) separately in boiling water till tender but NOT MUSHY. Put them all in a large bowl; add onion, red pepper, parsley & pepper. Pour over Vinaigrette & mix gently. Refrigerate to allow flavors to "marry". Serve. ♥

Vinaigrette

½ c. olive oil   4 cloves garlic, minced
¾ c. red wine vinegar   2 tsp. oregano
1 tsp. dry mustard   salt & pepper (opt.)

Whisk all ingredients together; pour over Bean Salad. ♥

EGGPLANT SALAD
with Yogurt Dressing
Serves Four

Fresh & tangy & just a little bit different ♥.

Yogurt Dressing (see below)
1 med. eggplant
salt
olive oil

1 bunch watercress
1 bunch red leaf lettuce
minced chives for garnish

Make the Yogurt Dressing & refrigerate. Peel & thinly slice eggplant. Sprinkle it with salt & let stand ½ hour (removes bitterness). Rinse in cool water & pat dry. Sauté in hot oil until crisp; drain on paper towels. Put watercress & lettuce leaves (any greens will do, but the more interesting, the better) on individual salad dishes; arrange eggplant on top & spoon over Yogurt Dressing. Sprinkle on chives & serve. ♥

Yogurt Dressing

1 c. plain yogurt
2 Tbsp. olive oil
1 tsp. garlic powder
½ tsp. basil
juice of 1 lemon

Mix all ingredients together & beat well. Cover & refrigerate. ♥

PRESSED FLOWERS
♥ Gifts from your garden ♥

Pressed flowers are so pretty and delicate and they can add a special touch to so many things. ♥ I have a huge old dictionary that I put my flowers in ~ ones that I grow and ones that I find wild in the woods. ♥ I love to include a tiny stem in my letters ❀ ~ To my friends on the West Coast who don't see the wild colors of the fall foliage, I send envelopes of leaves at the height of their color. ♥ Have you ever opened a book and found, between the pages, a tiny pressed flower? It's such a nice surprise! ♥ To make these placecards, dry the flowers flat &, using a toothpick, put a tiny bit of Elmer's glue on the back of the flower ~ glue to placecards. ♥ I love to sit in front of a fire on a cold stormy day and play with these slightly faded memories of summer. It just makes me feel good. ♥ Try it for yourself and for all those lucky people that you love. ♥

VEGETABLES

"Eat your vegetables!"
~Mom~

KITCHEN GARDENS

When most of us think of a garden we imagine the rows and rows of different vegetables, each variety demanding its own special treatment. We should worry about the soil needs, possible use of insecticides, mulches, and the necessity for the right amount of space. Then comes V-Day ~ drop everything! The garden is UP! Time for picking, digging, canning, drying and replanting. I don't know about you, but this is not my idea of a fun summer. ♥ But there is another type of garden that I do like to grow, which gives me the lovely satisfaction of having fresh food to serve without the intense amount of work involved in a large garden. I call it my "Kitchen Garden". ♥

I found a small plot of ground right outside my kitchen door, a perfect place for running out to pick a few herbs, some leaves of lettuce, or a tomato or two. I planted my favorite herbs ~ parsley, basil, camomile, dill, tarragon, mint, thyme and rosemary ~ then, two tomato plants, six heads of leaf lettuce (you don't pick the whole thing at once, just a leaf at a time as needed), radishes, some garlic and chives and flowers to fill in. I did take the time to prepare the soil, but since it was such a small area, it didn't take long at all and was well worth the trouble. After that I went right to the nursery and bought "starts," small plants all ready for planting ~ it took ½ hour to plant everything. ♥ Oh! One more thing, if you live where winters are mild, do include a dwarf lemon

68

tree in your Kitchen Garden ~ Imagine! Fresh lemons right outside your kitchen door! Anyway ~ the only "insecticide" I used was the interspersing of marigolds among the vegetables and herbs to deter certain types of bugs. The garlic and chives also help to control pests. After that, all I had to do was water ~ and for my trouble I had perfectly fresh salads every day, and lovely herbs to use in everything imaginable, including camomile flowers to boil for steam facials, and fresh flowers for my little vases.

So, if you only have a little space, or you've never gardened before, I suggest you try a Kitchen Garden of your own. ♥ It's fun, and easy and very rewarding. ♥

"We are rarely ill, and if we are, we go off somewhere and eat grass until we feel better." ♥
Paul Gallico

STUFFED ZUCCHINI

350° Serves Six

This has so many healthy ingredients and tastes so good that sometimes I make it a meal all by itself ~ and go to bed skinny!

3 medium zucchini
1 green pepper, chopped
2 tomatoes, chopped
1 onion, finely chopped
1 clove garlic, minced
½ c. parsley, minced

1 tsp. oregano
juice of ½ lemon
salt & pepper
1½ c. vegetable juice
2 c. grated jack cheese
3 slices sourdough toast

Preheat oven to 350°. Cut the zucchini in half length~ wise. Hollow out the zucchini by scooping out the pulp, reserving the shells. Chop the pulp & put it in a large skillet along with green pepper, tomatoes, onion, garlic, parsley, oregano, lemon juice, salt and pepper to taste, and ¾ c. of the vegetable juice. Cook slowly till vegetables are soft.   Pile the mixture into the zucchini shells. Distribute the cheese equally over the tops. Cube the toast & put the pieces on top of the stuffing. Put the zucchini in a baking pan & pour the remaining ¾ c. vegetable juice around them. Bake 30 minutes. Spoon hot juice over. ♥

70

GLAZED CARROTS

Serves Six

Bright orange color & a shimmer of glaze ~ They look best cut on the diagonal. ♥ Complimentary to almost any dinner. ♥

1½ lb. carrots, cut into 2" pieces
2 Tbsp. butter
½ c. brown sugar
2 c. orange juice, fresh is best ♥
⅛ tsp. orange zest
1¼ Tbsp. cornstarch
pinch of ginger

Peel the carrots & steam them just to tender crisp; set aside. In saucepan combine butter, sugar, orange juice & orange zest. Heat mixture until it begins to bubble ~ whisk in cornstarch & cook over medium heat until thickened. Add ginger & carrots to saucepan ~ stir gently ~ pour into serving dish. ♥

"One honest John Tompkins, a hedger and ditcher,
 Although he was poor, did not want to be richer;
 For all such vain wishes in him were prevented
 By a fortunate habit of being contented." ♥
 ♥ Jane Taylor

SPRING MEDLEY
Serves Six

I _love_ this dish — it's quick, easy, elegant & delicious — my four favorite things in cooking ♥

½ c. butter
3 bunches of radishes, sliced
4 bunches of watercress
squeeze of lemon juice
freshly ground pepper
Parmesan cheese (opt.)

Melt half the butter in a large skillet; sauté the radishes until almost tender (but still crisp), 4~5 min. Remove to serving dish. Remove the large tough stems from the watercress & sauté it in the remaining butter just till wilted ~ 2 to 3 min. Put the radishes back into the skillet with the watercress; add freshly ground pepper & a squeeze of lemon juice. Heat through, pour into serving dish & add a sprinkle of Parmesan cheese if you like. ♥ I have also made this with spinach when I couldn't get watercress & it was very good. ♥

Garden tip: plant nasturtiums amongst radishes — they deter pests & radishes love them. ♥

HOT CHERRY TOMATOES
Serves Four

A colorful side dish — easy & quick to make — but still an elegant accompaniment for almost any main course. ♥

2 Tbsp. butter
1 Tbsp. olive oil
1 clove garlic, minced
1 basket med. cherry tomatoes
2 Tbsp. fresh basil, minced ~ Or,
2 Tbsp. fresh parsley, minced

Melt butter & oil in large skillet. Add minced garlic. Over medium heat, add cherry tomatoes. Heat through ~ if skins begin to split, they are definitely done. Sprinkle on basil or parsley ~ stir & pour into serving dish. ♥

ASPARAGUS ON TOAST

A delicious & different way to serve asparagus. ♥

Lay spears of tender cooked asparagus on a toasted slice of bread. Sprinkle over about 1 Tbsp. of the water asparagus was cooked in. Pour melted butter over all & serve. ♥

TOMATO CAULIFLOWER CASSEROLE

375° Serves Six

A hearty casserole with a lovely crusty topping. ♥

1 cauliflower washed & separated into bite~sized pieces
6 tomatoes peeled, seeded, & chopped
½ c. melted butter
freshly ground pepper
½ c. Parmesan cheese
⅓ c. bread crumbs
1 c. grated Muenster cheese
½ c. minced parsley

Preheat oven to 375° Steam the cauliflower just until tender ~ reserve.
Dip each tomato into boiling water for about 35 seconds and peel
off the skin with your fingers. Cut them in half, squeeze out the
juice & seeds, and chop coarsely. Butter a casserole, put in the
cauliflower flowerets, layer the tomatoes on top, and pepper to
taste. Dribble half the butter over the top. Combine cheeses,
breadcrumbs, & parsley in a bowl & sprinkle evenly over casserole.
Dribble over remaining butter and bake 30 minutes until browned.
Serve hot. ♥

" The Greeks had just one word for 'economize'.
Our New England grandmothers had twelve:
' Eat it up; use it up; make do, or do without.' "
♥ Helen Adamson ♥

PURÉED VEGETABLES

Sometimes you need a dish with a special texture to round out your menu. Either of these can fill the bill. They both have bright color, smooth texture & delicious flavor. ♥

Carrot Purée

Serves Four

5 medium carrots, sliced
2 Tbsp. butter, melted
2 Tbsp. rum

5-6 Tbsp. heavy cream
salt & pepper, to taste

Preheat oven to 350°. Wash and slice the carrots. Cook them in boiling water till tender; set aside. Melt butter in a small saucepan, stir in rum & 5 Tbsp. cream ~ heat till steaming, but don't boil. Put the carrots in a food processor, add butter sauce & whirl to smooth consistancy. Add additional Tbsp. of cream if you think it needs it. Stir in salt & pepper; remove to heat-proof dish & reheat in oven for 10-15 min. Serve. ♥

Puréed Peas

Serves Four

1 10 oz. pkg. frozen peas
2 slices bacon, chopped
1/3 c. water

2 Tbsp. butter
5 Tbsp. heavy cream
salt & pepper, to taste

Put the peas & bacon in a small saucepan with 1/3 c. water. Cover & cook till peas are tender; drain. Put the peas (with the bacon) in the food processor; add the butter & cream & whirl till smooth. Put the peas through a fine mesh sieve to remove skins (of peas). Add salt & pepper to taste. Reheat in 350° oven for 15 min. till hot. Serve. ♥

GREEN BEANS
AND ONIONS

Serves Four

It's the wine vinegar that turns this into something special.

1 lb. young green beans
1 chopped onion
2 Tbsp. butter
salt and pepper
½ tsp. wine vinegar
finely chopped parsley

Snap off stems and tips of beans; leave them whole. Cook them in boiling water until tender, but still firm. Drain them. In a heavy saucepan slowly sauté the onion in the butter until soft and golden. Add the green beans, mix well, and reheat over low flame for a few minutes. Add salt and pepper to taste, then the vinegar. Sprinkle with chopped parsley before serving. ♥

"I am not a gourmet chick." ♥ Pearl Bailey

CREAM CHEESE POTATOES

Serves Eight

I always make these for Thanksgiving ♥. If you have any leftovers, they'll keep in your refrigerator for 2 weeks and they are so good formed into patties, dipped in flour, and fried in butter ♥.

9 large potatoes, peeled and halved
2 3-oz. pkgs. cream cheese
1 c. sour cream
2 tsp. onion salt
1 tsp. salt
½ tsp. pepper
3 Tbsp. butter

Cook potatoes in boiling, salted water until tender. Mash them until smooth. Add the remaining ingredients and beat till light and fluffy ♥.

"I hate guests who complain of the cooking and leave bits and pieces all over the place and cream cheese sticking to the mirrors."

Colette, Chéri 1920 ♥

TWICE-BAKED POTATOES

350° Serves Six

These potatoes can turn an ordinary meal into something special with very little extra work. ♥

6 medium baking potatoes
1 8oz. pkg. cream cheese
½ c. hot milk
1 tsp. onion salt
2 Tbsp. butter
Freshly ground pepper
½ c. parsley, finely chopped
paprika

Put cream cheese out to soften. Scrub potatoes and dry. Grease them with butter & salt the skins. Bake at 350° for 1 hour. Remove from oven & cool to handle. Cut them in half lengthwise ~ remove cooked potato to bowl, being careful to reserve skins whole. Mash with cream cheese, hot milk, onion salt, butter, & pepper. Pile mixture back into skins. Sprinkle with paprika & parsley & bake 20 min. more. ♥

78

· PESTO ·

Pesto, to me, is like "green gold". Here on the Vineyard I grow
basil in the summer, make and freeze pesto to have all
winter long. It is delicious on pasta, on sliced garden
tomatoes, or in soups. For an appetizer I once hollowed
out cherry tomatoes and filled them with pesto. ♥ ♥ ♥ ♥ ♥

2 c. fresh basil   dash of pepper
3 Tbsp. pine nuts   ½ c. Parmesan cheese
2 cloves garlic   ¼ c. Romano cheese
½ tsp. salt   ⅔ c. olive oil
                                    2 Tbsp. butter

To prepare: Toast the pinenuts in a small skillet in a bit
of butter. Cut the Parmesan & Romano into one-inch squares
and grate separately in your food processor ~ measure out.
Wash and drain basil ~ remove stems. Put all ingredients
into food processor and blend until smooth. Freeze or
refrigerate until ready to use. ♥

79

POTATO CROQUETTES

350° Serves Six to Eight

To the true potato connoisseur, no amount of work is too much in the quest for potato perfection ♥.

8 med. russet potatoes	4 slices bacon
2 eggs, beaten	½ c. onion, minced
3 Tbsp. heavy cream	½ c. milk
salt & pepper, to taste	2 eggs, beaten
¼ tsp. nutmeg	½ c. unbleached flour
½ c. cheddar cheese, grated	3 c. bread crumbs
2 Tbsp. chives, minced	oil for frying
2 Tbsp. parsley, minced	sour cream

Bake potatoes for 1 hour at 350°. Cool to handle. Scoop potato pulp into a large bowl & mash well. (Reserve skins for eating later!) Stir beaten eggs into potatoes & add cream to hold pulp together. Add salt, pepper, nutmeg, cheese, chives & parsley & stir well. Fry bacon till crisp (reserve grease); cool & crumble over potatoes. Pour out all but 1 Tbsp. bacon fat & sauté onion in fat, slowly, till soft. Add the onions to the potato mixture & stir well. Form the potatoes into little balls or cylinders. Mix together milk & eggs in a small bowl. Roll each croquette in flour; dip them in egg mixture & then into bread crumbs. Put about 1" oil into large skillet over med. high heat. Fry croquettes until well browned & put them on a cookie sheet. Bake them at 350° for about six minutes. Serve hot with sour cream on the side. ♥

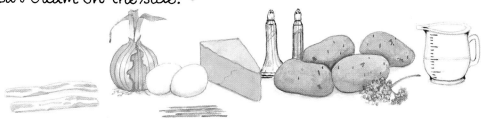

FILLED TOMATOES

400° ❤ Serves six

They're crisped on top, the stuffing is moist and flavorful ~ and they go with almost everything. Perfect with fish, perfect with beef ~ even perfect with scrambled eggs for breakfast!

- 6 firm, ripe tomatoes
- 2 cloves mashed, minced garlic
- 5 Tbsp. minced parsley
- 4 Tbsp. minced green onion
- ¼ tsp. thyme
- ¼ tsp. salt
- freshly ground pepper
- ⅓ c. olive oil
- ¾ c. plain dry bread crumbs

Preheat oven to 400°. Cut the tomatoes in half and gently squeeze out the juice and seeds. Lightly salt and pepper the halves. Blend all remaining ingredients and taste to correct seasoning. Fill each tomato half & sprinkle with a few drops of olive oil. Arrange tomatoes in roasting pan, and bake in upper third of your oven for 12 minutes or until filling is golden brown. ❤ These can be made ahead and cooked when needed. ❤

SPINACH SOUFFLÉ

350° Serves Four

Wonderful texture and flavor ~ a good complement to an icy cold Gazpacho with shrimp. ♥

1 c. cottage cheese
1 3oz. pkg. cream cheese, softened
2 eggs
3 Tbsp. flour
2 Tbsp. melted butter
3/4 tsp. salt
1/8 tsp. each nutmeg & pepper
1 10oz. pkg. spinach, thawed & drained

Place all ingredients except spinach in blender. Blend well. Combine spinach with cheese mixture and pour into a buttered quart soufflé dish. Set dish in a pan of hot water. Bake in a 350° oven for 70 minutes, or until set in center. ♥

CHILI CASSEROLE

350° Serves Six

A delicious dish to serve in a vegetarian dinner ~ perfect with Chicken Enchiladas (p. 94). ♥

5 4oz. cans whole, mild green chiles
3 c. Jack cheese, thinly sliced
1 c. milk
4 eggs

3 Tbsp. unbleached flour
freshly ground pepper
3 c. Cheddar cheese, grated
2 Tbsp. parsley or cilantro

Preheat oven to 350°. Slit chilies open & mop with paper towels to remove excess moisture. Stuff each chili with a slice of Jack cheese & place them in ungreased baking dish. Whisk together milk, eggs, flour & pepper to taste and pour over chilies. Sprinkle grated cheese over the top & bake 45 min. Remove from oven, sprinkle minced parsley or cilantro over the casserole & Serve. ♥

POTATO PACKAGES

350° Serves Six

These are great to serve at barbecues ~ Everyone gets a package. ♥

6 lg. baking potatoes, cubed
12 Tbsp. chopped onion
6 Tbsp. minced parsley

6 Tbsp. heavy cream
6 Tbsp. butter
salt & pepper to taste

Preheat oven to 350°. Lay out 6 large pieces of aluminum foil & evenly divide potatoes among them. Sprinkle each with 2 Tbsp. onion, 1 Tbsp. parsley, 1 Tbsp. cream. Dot each with 1 Tbsp. butter; s & p to taste. Wrap tightly ~ put on cookie sheet; bake 45 min. Serve. ♥

"Like a good pioneer, father hankered to eat outdoors. And he ate outdoors, come gale, come zephyr. . . . Outdoors put an edge on my father like that on a new-filed saw. . . .

"Beyond the cook-house, under the oaks that dipped their eastern leaves in the ocean, father built him a table, with benches all the way around it, and mother had to serve our meals there. The wind blew up the tablecloth. We had to anchor it down with big stones. Things cooled off. The tea went flat and chilled. Ants got into the sugar. Fuzzy caterpillers dropped into our milk. Bees got into the syrup and into father's trousers. Bees stung father. But eat out under the sky he would. . . .

"I can see father and all of us out there under the oaks even yet. A dozen of us round one table. Girls with honey-colored hair flowing in the wind, little boys' spiralled curls ruffling up. Golden bumble bees blazing past. A stiff breeze up. Butterflies lighting on the rim of the milk-pitcher. The sunlight making polka dots on our noses and the tablecloth, as it spilled down through the oak leaves. The whole deep sky blue above us, dappled with fair-weather clouds. . . . Seagulls leaning white on the wind. And father with his big brown moustache all one way in the wind, the wind in his blue eyes, making them twinkle. Father smiling and eating hugely and shouting out between mouthfuls —
'Yes, Sir! This is the way to live! Out in the air, out where a man belongs!' "

Robert P. Tristram Coffin ♥

MAIN DISHES

"Several years ago 'Life' had a picture story on how to skin an eel . . . . I trust everyone cut it out and put it in his files."

♥ James Beard ♥

COLD SALMON WITH WATERCRESS AIOLI

Serves Six

A beautiful make-ahead dish ~ the colors are subtle, the flavors delightful. Serve it with Spring Medley (p.72). ♥

1 whole egg
2 egg yolks
3 Tbsp. fresh lemon juice
2 tsp. Dijon mustard
2 cloves garlic
½ c. olive oil

½ c. vegetable oil
½ c. watercress, leaves only
½ c. fresh dill
Freshly ground pepper & salt, to taste
2½ lbs. fresh salmon

Put the egg, egg yolks, lemon juice, mustard & garlic into food processor & blend 1 minute. Blend the olive & vegetable oils together, then, with machine running, pour in the oil in a very slow steady stream. Add watercress & dill to sauce & whirl to blend well~ sauce will be light green. Add freshly ground pepper & salt to taste. Chill. Remove skin & bones from salmon (tweezers work very well for the bones). Place the salmon on a rack set into a large skillet with a cover. Add about an inch of water to the pan, cover & steam about 10 min. till fish begins to flake. Re~ move to your refrigerator & chill. When ready, put salmon on serving plates, spoon over about 3~4 Tbsp. of sauce for each & serve. ♥

APPLES, SWEET POTATOES, WITH PORK CHOPS

400° Serves Six

The wonderful thing about this recipe is that your whole delicious dinner is made in one dish. ♥ It's perfect for a cold wintry day ♥

6 lg. sweet potatoes
4 Tbsp. cooking oil
6 2" thick pork chops
salt and pepper

Stuffing
6 lg. tart apples
1 c. golden raisins
1 tsp. cinnamon

Preheat oven to 400°. Peel the potatoes; cut them into large chunks & boil them till they're about half-done. Set aside. Heat the oil and brown the chops quickly on both sides ~ salt & pepper. Remove and cool. Make the stuffing. Cut a deep slit in the side of each chop & fill with the stuffing. Put the stuffed chops & the sweet potatoes into a large baking pan. Peel, halve & core the apples. Place them in the pan with the chops & potatoes & sprinkle on the raisins. Sprinkle cinnamon on each apple. Cover the pan tightly with foil and bake 50 minutes until apples & chops are tender. ♥

Stuffing

1 cube butter
1 med. onion, finely chopped
3 ribs celery, chopped
½ c. parsley, minced
2 c. dry bread crumbs
salt and pepper
♥

Melt butter ~ add onion and celery and cook slowly till soft. Add parsley, bread crumbs, and salt & pepper. Mix well and correct consistency with more bread crumbs or butter. ♥

FILET MIGNON IN PHYLLO WITH MADEIRA SAUCE

400° Serves Six

This makes a gorgeous presentation in the beautifully browned phyllo. ♥

3 lbs. filet mignon steaks, 2 in. thick
4 Tbsp. butter
1 lb. mushrooms, minced & dried
4 shallots, minced
1 pkg. phyllo pastry
½ c. butter, melted
Madeira Sauce (recipe below)

The Victim

Preheat oven to 400°. Trim the fat off the meat. Quickly brown the filets in 2 Tbsp. butter over high heat. Set aside. Melt remaining butter in the same pan & sauté the mushrooms & shallots for 4-5 min., till soft. Remove from heat. Layer 12 sheets of phyllo together, brushing each layer with melted butter. (Phyllo dries out quickly~ keep unused portion covered.) Spread ½ the mushroom mixture on pastry & put the beef on top. Cover beef with remaining mushrooms. Fold the phyllo around the beef. Prepare 6 more sheets of pastry; brush each with butter. Seal all edges with additional pastry & brush top with butter. Place beef in buttered baking pan & bake for 30 min. till pastry is browned. Serve with:

Madeira Sauce

3 Tbsp. butter
1½ Tbsp. flour
3/4 c. beef stock

1 tsp. Kitchen Bouquet
¼ c. Madeira wine
freshly ground pepper

Melt butter, stir in flour, cook 5 min. Add beef stock, Kitchen Bouquet & Madeira. Cook until thickened; stir in pepper to taste. ♥

ORIENTAL FISH

Serves Four

Tender fish filets steamed in an Oriental sauce. ♥ Quick & easy ~ low-calorie & delicious. ♥

4 fish filets: flounder, sole, yellowtail
1 carrot, julienned
3 green onions with tops, julienned
    fresh ginger, to taste
2 Tbsp. parsley, minced (or 1 Tbsp. cilantro)
2 Tbsp. rice vinegar
2 Tbsp. light soy sauce
1 Tbsp. lemon juice
2 tsp. sesame oil

Lay the filets on a heat-proof plate ~ spread vegies over the top. Mix together vinegar, soy sauce, lemon juice & sesame oil; pour mixture over the fish. Into a large deep skillet put a Pyrex lid or another heat-proof plate ~ something the fish plate can sit on & be off the bottom. Add an inch or so of water to the skillet. Put the plate of fish into the pan. Cover & steam 7-10 min. Serve. ♥ You can also roll the vegies up in the filets & cook them that way. Try fresh snow peas & steamed new potatoes with this dish. ♥

"Take time for all things".
♥ Benjamin Franklin ♥

PASTA WITH SMOKED SALMON & PEAS

Serves Six

Light and summery ~ delicate flavors and colors blended to a delightful taste and texture. ♥ Begin with Vichyssoise (p.38), & serve the pasta with a crisp salad ~ finish with Kiwi Ice (p.129). ♥ Trust me, they'll love it ~ and you!

3/4 c. dry white wine
4 Tbsp. shallots, minced
1 1/4 c. heavy cream
8 oz. narrow egg noodles, dried

3/4 c. cooked peas
3 Tbsp. fresh dill, snipped
1/3 lb. smoked salmon, sliced
4 Tbsp. pine nuts, toasted

Toast the pine nuts in a small skillet with a Tbsp. of butter. Keep your eye on them ~ they burn easily. Set aside on paper towel to drain. Cook the peas & set aside. Put the white wine & shallots together in a small saucepan & bring to boil. Allow the wine to reduce by about a Tbsp. Stir in cream; bring to boil; simmer for 5~6 min. Cover the pan & remove from heat. Put the pasta into boiling water & cook just till tender; rinse in cool water; drain. Put the pasta into serving dish. Bring sauce back to boil ~ remove from heat ~ stir in peas & dill. Pour sauce over pasta; toss to coat. Add the thinly sliced strips of smoked salmon & the freshly toasted pine nuts ~ Toss gently & serve. ♥

♥ ♥ ♥

"We live in deeds, not years; in thoughts, not breaths; In feelings, not in figures on a dial. We should count time by heart~throbs. He most lives who thinks most ~ feels the noblest ~ acts the best."

P.J. Bailey ♥

CHICKEN BREASTS STUFFED with CHEESE

Serves Six 375°

Use plump breasts so you can get lots of cheese inside! This is such a favorite with one of my friends ~ he requests it every chance he gets! ♥

3 large chicken breasts, boned & halved
1 lb. jack cheese, sliced
4 eggs
3 Tbsp. minced parsley
3 Tbsp. freshly grated Parmesan cheese
salt & pepper
½ c. unbleached flour
4 Tbsp. olive oil
juice of ½ lemon

Preheat oven to 375° Carefully put a slit in the side of each breast-half with a sharp knife. Fill with as many slices of jack cheese as will comfortably fit. Fasten tightly with toothpicks so the cheese won't melt out while cooking. Mix together eggs, Parmesan cheese, and parsley. Roll the chicken in flour, coating heavily, and then dip in the egg mixture. Heat the oil in a large skillet over moderately high heat. Put the chicken in and pour the rest of the egg mixture over the top. Fry very quickly just to lightly brown. Place chicken in buttered baking pan ~ lay any extra cheese on tops and around sides of chicken. Bake 25 min.~ do not overcook. Remove toothpicks, squeeze lemon juice over, sprinkle on some parsley and serve. ♥

91

LEMON CHICKEN

Serves Six

One of the easiest, fastest "gourmet" dishes I know.
These chicken breasts melt in your mouth.
Serve them with buttered peas & stuffed tomatoes. ♥

3 whole chicken breasts, boned, skinned & halved
1½ c. unbleached flour
⅓ c. butter
2 Tbsp. olive oil
salt and pepper

Wash and dry chicken breasts. Pound them flat
with a mallet. Melt the butter and oil in a large
skillet. Put the flour in a plastic bag and drop the
breasts in to coat. Regulate the heat to moderately
high, and put the chicken breasts in the skillet.
Cook approx. 3 minutes on each side. When they
are done, salt & pepper them and put them on an
oven-proof dish and into a 250° oven to keep warm
while you make the sauce.

The Sauce:

Add 4 Tbsp. butter to the chicken skillet & melt,
scraping up brown bits in pan. Remove from heat;
add 4 Tbsp. finely chopped parsley, & the juice from
½ lemon. Pour hot sauce over breasts and serve. ♥

POULET AU POIRE CRÈME

400°   Serves Four

Tender chicken filets wrapped around a cornbread & hazelnut stuffing & sauced over with delicate pear cream ~ a wonderful dish. I think it's good served with a carrot & raisin salad & steamed asparagus. ♥

2 whole lg. chicken breasts, boned, skinned & halved

4 Tbsp. butter

1 shallot, minced

2 stalks celery, minced

4 green onions with tops, minced

½ tsp thyme

salt & pepper to taste

2 c. crumbled cornbread

½ c. toasted hazelnuts

I just use cornbread made from a mix. Toast the hazelnuts on a cookie sheet for 10 min. (till skins crack) in a 400° oven. Roll them between fingers to remove skins; chop very coarsely; set aside. Melt butter in skillet; sauté shallot, celery, onions & thyme till tender. Add cornbread, salt & pepper & hazelnuts. Add enough water so that mixture holds together ~ about 4 Tbsp. Set aside. Gently pound chicken breasts to ¼" thick. Put a handful of the cornbread mixture onto each breast & form the breast into a ball around the stuffing, seam down. Put them into a buttered baking dish ~ dot each with butter; add 2 Tbsp. water to the pan; cover & bake at 400° for 20~25 min. Pour the pear cream over the chicken & serve. ♥

PEAR CREAM

This sauce is also delicious on roasted duck. ♥

1 pint heavy cream

1 Tbsp. honey

1 1 lb. can Bartlett pears

Drain the pears. Bring the cream to a boil, lower heat to simmer ~ cook till cream is reduced by about ⅓ ~ about 5 min. Add honey & pears; cook 1~2 min. Purée sauce in food processor & serve. ♥ Use toasted chopped hazelnuts for garnish. ♥

CHICKEN ENCHILADAS

350° Serves Six

Have "Mexican Night" at your house. Serve these delicious enchiladas with a Chili Casserole (p.83) and some refried beans with chopped onion and melted cheese. And don't forget the Margaritas!

3 c. cooked chopped chicken
1 4 oz. can chopped green chilies
1 7 oz. can green chili salsa
3/4 tsp. salt

2½ c. heavy cream
1 doz. corn tortillas
2 c. grated Jack cheese
oil

Preheat oven to 350°. Mix together chicken, green chilies, & green chili salsa. In another fairly large bowl mix to~ gether cream and salt. Heat about 1 inch of oil in a small frying pan. Dip each tortilla into hot oil for about 3 seconds, just to soften. Drain on paper tow~ els and lay into bowl containing cream. Fill each tortilla with chicken mixture ~ roll them up and place into ungreased baking dish. Pour extra cream over the enchiladas and sprinkle on the cheese. Bake uncovered for 25 minutes and serve hot.

HOT STIR-FRIED SHRIMP

Serves Six

Use the extra-large shrimp for a spicy, delicious and elegant company dinner. ♥ It's nice served with cold artichokes and a crispy salad. ♥

24 large shrimp	10 Tbsp. cornstarch
5 Tbsp. peanut oil	10 Tbsp. sherry
8 green onions with tops, chopped	10 Tbsp. soy sauce
3 dried small red chilies, broken	1½ tsp. salt
2 lg. cloves garlic, crushed	2½ tsp. powdered ginger
2 Tbsp. fresh ginger root, crushed	4 c. hot cooked brown
½ c. water chestnuts, sliced	rice

Clean and butterfly the shrimp. In a medium-sized bowl combine 4 Tbsp. _each_ of the cornstarch, sherry and soy sauce. Add 1 tsp. of the salt & 1 tsp. powdered ginger. Put in the shrimp & marinate in the mixture for 20 minutes. Heat peanut oil in wok until very hot. Add crushed fresh ginger and garlic & cook until brown. Discard ginger & garlic but keep the oil in the wok. Drain shrimp, reserve marinade. To the reserved marinade add the remaining 6 Tbsp. _each_ of the cornstarch, sherry & soy sauce, the remaining ½ tsp. salt & 1½ tsp. powdered ♥ ginger. In hot oil stir-fry shrimp for 2 min. till opaque. Add green onions & dried peppers. Cook 1 min. Add marinade & water chestnuts & cook 3 min. till sauce thickens ~ Do not overcook shrimp. Serve over hot rice. ♥

95

RICE AND SOUR CREAM CASSEROLE

350° Serves Six

This is a wonderful dish to serve to your vegetarian friends, healthy and filling. The cheese makes a good crusty top. ♥

1 c. uncooked brown rice

3 med. zucchini, sliced

1 7½ oz. can chopped green chilies

12 oz. jack cheese, grated

2 lg. tomatoes, thinly sliced

2 c. sour cream

1 tsp. oregano

1 tsp. garlic salt

¼ c. chopped green pepper

¼ c. chopped green onion

2 Tbsp. chopped fresh parsley

Cook the rice. Layer in large buttered casserole: cooked rice, chopped chilies, ½ of the cheese, zucchini and tomato slices. Combine the sour cream, oregano, garlic salt, green pepper, and green onion. Spoon this mixture over the tomatoes and sprinkle on the rest of the cheese. Bake at 350° for 45 minutes. Sprinkle with fresh parsley. Serve either as main course or as a side dish. ♥

VEAL BIRDS

350° Serves Six

This is one of my favorite recipes for a special dinner. Try it with hot homemade applesauce — maybe for Valentines Day. ♥

2½ lbs. veal cutlets
2½ c. stuffing, your own, or p. 87
1½ Tbsp. oil
3 Tbsp. butter
freshly ground pepper

salt, to taste
2 c. chicken broth
½ lb. mushrooms, thickly sliced
3/4 c. heavy cream
5 slices bacon, crisply fried

Preheat oven to 350°. Trim fat off veal & pound with mallet till ¼" thick. Cut into pieces about 5" x 6". Put stuffing down the middle of each cutlet & roll into little packages; tie with string. Melt oil & butter in large skillet and brown birds very quickly. Put them in a single layer into a casserole, surround with sliced mushrooms, pour chicken broth over, cover tightly, and bake 35 min. Pour in the cream, remove the cover, and bake 30 min. more. Remove from oven, sprinkle on crumbled bacon, and serve. ♥ For applesauce recipe see page 141. ♥

REAL BIRDS

HERB ROASTED CHICKEN

425° Serves Four

A heavenly roasted chicken flavored with herbs; brown, juicy, and crisp-skinned. Serve with Potato Croquettes (p.80) and, for dessert, luscious Baked Bananas (p.147). ♥

1 large roasting chicken (about 6 lbs.)	3/4 tsp. thyme leaves
3 Tbsp. butter, softened	3/4 tsp. basil leaves
1 clove garlic, minced	
3 Tbsp. grated Parmesan cheese	6 Tbsp. butter, softened
1/2 tsp. sage leaves	salt

Preheat oven to 425° Wash chicken inside & out; pat dry. Cream together 3 Tbsp. butter, garlic, Parmesan, sage, thyme and basil. This mixture goes under the skin, so turn the chicken breast-side-up and work your fingers under skin at the openings on each side of the breast. Continue onto thigh and leg & make the skin as loose as possible. Using fingers, spread herb mixture evenly under skin. Smear 3 Tbsp. butter both inside the chicken & on the outside of the skin. Put the chicken, breast up, in a roasting pan and then into the oven. Melt remaining butter; Cook chicken 15 min., basting once. Lower heat to 350° Roast for about 20 min. per lb., basting with melted butter every 10 min. Chicken is done when the leg moves easily in its socket, & juices are clear yellow when pierced with fork. Allow chicken to sit 10 min. before carving. Serve. ♥

PAN-FRIED CHICKEN
& CREAM GRAVY

Serves Four

Indulge yourself for an old-time Sunday dinner. Have it at four o'clock on a nippy fall day and don't forget the mashed potatoes, ♥ hot biscuits with butter and honey ~ Delicious! For Best Biscuits recipe, see p. 140.

For Best Biscuits recipe, see p. 140.

3 lb. chicken in 8 pieces	1 tsp. salt
Milk	½ tsp. pepper
1 c. flour	Frying oil

Wash and dry the chicken pieces. Put in a shallow dish with milk to cover for 1 hour. Mix the flour, salt and pepper in a plastic bag. Drop the milk ~ soaked chicken in the bag and shake well. Heat ½ inch oil in large skillet to medium ~ high and put the dark meat in first. Five minutes later add the whitemeat and fry for 25 minutes, turning often with tongs. Remove, drain on paper towels and keep warm while you make the:

Cream Gravy   ♥ ♥ ♥

3 Tbsp. pan drippings and butter	1½ c. cream
3 Tbsp. flour	salt and pepper

Heat the pan drippings and butter and scrape up any brown bits in the pan. Stir in the flour and blend, over low heat. Slowly add cream, stirring con~ stantly, until smooth. Add salt & pepper; cook 7 minutes.

LINGUINI IN WHITE CLAM SAUCE

Serves Four

You can keep the ingredients for this easy dish in your pantry ~ and you'll always be ready for unexpected guests. ♥ Try it with a spinach salad (p. 53), garlic bread & steamed baby carrots. ♥ ♥ This dish can be used as a side dish for something extra special. ♥

½ c. butter
¼ c. olive oil
2 cloves garlic, minced
2 7½ oz. cans chopped clams
1 bottle clam juice
½ c. finely chopped parsley
½ lb. linguini, fresh is best
1 doz. fresh small clams, opt.
Freshly grated Parmesan cheese

Heat butter and oil, add garlic and cook slowly until golden. Drain the clams ~ reserve the liquid and add enough bottled clam juice to make 2 cups. Stir the liquid into the butter mixture and simmer, uncovered, for 10 minutes. Add chopped clams, parsley, & salt and pepper & heat through. Cook the linguini in boiling water till just tender. Pour the sauce over. If using fresh clams (a nice touch, but not necessary) boil a small amount of water, add clams, cover, and steam just until they open. Arrange them around pasta and pour the sauce over all. Pass the Parmesan cheese and enjoy ♥.
Tips: When you buy clams or mussels, make sure the shells are tightly closed. The best Parmeson cheese is Reggiano, expensive ~ but, do a taste test ! ♥

SCALLOPS IN PUFF PASTRY

450° Serves Four

Asparagus & fresh scallops in scallop shells baked with a top crust of puff pastry & finished with Citrus Butter. ♥

1 bunch of asparagus
2 Tbsp. butter
2 Tbsp. sherry
4 large scallop shells

1½ lbs. scallops
about ½ lb. puff pastry
1 egg, beaten
Citrus Butter

Make Citrus Butter (recipe below). Preheat oven to 450° Break tough ends off asparagus & discard. Slice the spears into ½" diagonal pieces. Sauté them in butter for 2 min. over medium high heat. Add sherry & stir 1 min. more. Remove from heat & divide asparagus evenly between the 4 scallop shells~ then divide the uncooked scallops between the shells. Roll out the puff pastry to ¼" thick. Lay a small plate on the dough & cut around to fit over scallop shells. Lay the circles of puff pastry over the shells & seal tightly over edges. Brush beaten egg over entire pastry, including edges. Bake 10~15 min. until golden brown. Cut open center & add a melon baller full of Citrus Butter ~ serve. ♥

CITRUS BUTTER

½ c. butter, softened
juice of 1 lime
juice of 1 lemon

juice of ½ orange
1 tsp. each of julienne zest
of lime, lemon & orange

Blanche the zest (to take out the bitterness); strain. Cream all ingredients together; chill. ♥

ROAST WILD DUCK GLAZE

Makes 1½ cups

We brushed this glaze over wild duck breasts last Thanksgiving and they were wonderful. ♥

- 1 c. apricot preserves
- ½ c. honey
- 1 Tbsg. brandy
- 1 Tbsp. Cointreau
- 1 tsp. freshly grated lemon rind

Mix ingredients together. Pour over oven-roasted wild ducks about 15 minutes before they are done. ♥

SHRIMPS IN WHITE WINE AND CREAM

Serves Four

Just reading the ingredients in this dish makes my mouth water ~ it has one of the most elegant sauces I've ever tasted ~ the flaming brandy puts on quite a show. Be sure not to overcook the shrimp. I like to serve it alongside of tiny steamed new potatoes, or over hot pasta, with a side dish of stuffed tomatoes.

3 Tbsp. butter
1 minced shallot
1½ lbs. large shrimp
pinch of thyme
1 bay leaf
salt and pepper
2 Tbsp. brandy

3/4 c. dry white wine
1 c. cream
2 egg yolks
1 tsp. lemon juice
1 tsp. chopped parsley
1 tsp. chervil
1 tsp. tarragon

Shell and devein the shrimp. In a heavy saucepan sauté the minced shallot in the butter until golden. Add the shrimp, pinch of thyme, 1 bay leaf, and a little salt & pepper. Simmer the shrimp for 5 minutes, turning occasionally. Warm the brandy, light it, and pour it flaming over the shrimp. Shake the pan back & forth until the flame dies, then add 3/4 c. white wine. Simmer the shrimp for 5 minutes more & transfer them to a heated serving dish; keep them warm. Reduce the pan juices to ⅓ their original quantity. Mix together 1 c. of cream, 2 egg yolks, 1 tsp. each of lemon juice, parsley, chervil & tarragon. Add this to the pan, and after it thickens slightly, do not let it boil; pour the hot sauce over the shrimp.

CORNISH GAME HENS
350° Serves Four

Wild rice, toasted nuts, a hint of orange, & sweet hoisin sauce make for interesting flavors & textures ~ the marinade browns beautifully ♥.

¼ c. sherry
½ c. hoisin sauce
3 Tbsp. toasted sesame oil
zest of 1 orange, blanched
2 large game hens

¾ c. wild rice
1½ c. chicken broth
½ c. hazelnuts
3 Tbsp. butter
2 shallots, chopped

Mix together sherry, hoisin sauce, sesame oil & the blanched zest of an orange, minced. (Blanching removes bitterness) Wash & dry the hens. Rub the mixture all over birds, inside & out. Pour remaining mixture over hens ~ cover & refrigerate for at least 3 hours (overnight is O.K.) Periodically brush the birds with marinade. About 2 hours before you plan to serve, simmer the rice in chicken broth for about 45 min., till tender. Meanwhile put the nuts on a cookie sheet & toast them in a 350° oven for about 30 min., till browned. Chop very coarsely. Melt butter in heavy skillet; add shallots & toasted nuts. Sauté slowly until butter is browned (not blackened); add rice, stir for about 2 min. & remove from heat. Stuff the hens with rice mixture; place them breast side up in baking dish & bake at 350° for 45~50 min. Mix remaining marin~ ade with remaining rice ~ put mixture in buttered baking dish & then into oven for last 15 min. of baking time. Split the hens & serve them on a bed of rice. ♥

PAUPIETTES WITH BEURRE BLANC

400°   Serves Six

When you unmold these you have a perfect little circle of steamed fish wrapped around a center of spinach stuffing. Sauced over lightly with the beurre blanc & served with Glazed Carrots (p. 71) they make a pretty delectable picture. ♥ Try Tomato Soup (p. 36) to start & Cheesecake (p. 115) for dessert. ♥

2 c. fresh spinach, blanched
10 mushrooms, chopped
1 onion, finely chopped
2 cloves garlic, minced

6 Tbsp. butter
freshly ground pepper
dash nutmeg
1½ lbs. filets of flounder

Preheat oven to 400° Finely chop the blanched spinach & set aside. Sauté mushrooms, onion & garlic in 3 Tbsp. butter; add pepper to taste & just a pinch of nutmeg; cook, stirring, till butter melts; remove from heat. Butter six 6 oz. ramekins. Score the darker side of the fish with a sharp knife & cut into pieces to line the ramekins, putting the scored side toward the inside Fill lined ramekins with spinach mixture. Cover with foil & place them in roasting pan. Pour boiling water into roasting pan — about 1" deep. Bake for 16 minutes. Remove from oven; drain off juices from ramekins and unmold onto serving dishes. Cover lightly with beurre blanc. ♥

Beurre Blanc

¼ c. dry white wine
¼ c. white wine vinegar
3 Tbsp. shallots, chopped

1½ c. COLD butter
2 Tbsp. parsley, minced
salt & pepper, to taste

Boil wine, vinegar & shallots; reduce to 1-2 Tbsp. Turn heat VERY low. Whisking constantly, slowly add COLD butter, one Tbsp. at a time. Sauce will thicken — add parsley, salt & pepper. Pour over paupiettes. ♥

MY GRANDMA'S TURKEY STUFFING

For a 20 lb. bird

I guess you could say this is the old-fashioned way to make stuffing — my great-grandmother also made it this way ♥. It's so moist and you can change it any way you like with additions of your own, but we like it plain & simple. ♥

2 loaves white bread, dried
1 loaf wheat bread, dried
2 sticks butter
2 or 3 onions, chopped
6 stalks celery, chopped
1 jar sage leaves
1 Tbsp. salt or to taste
freshly ground pepper

Set the bread out to dry a couple of days before you make the stuffing. ♥ Put about 6 in. of the hottest water you can stand to touch into your clean sink. Dip each slice of bread into the water; wring it out well & put it into a large bowl. The bread will be kind of chunky, doughy, chewy — melt butter in a large skillet. Very slowly, sauté the onions & celery in the butter until soft — do not brown the butter. Meanwhile, over the sink, rub the sage leaves between your fingers & remove woody stems — put the leaves in with the bread. Pour the butter mixture over the bread & mix well with your hands (but don't burn yourself!). Add about 1 Tbsp. salt — it needs lots of salt, so they say ♥, & then add pepper to taste. Now for the tasting, the tasting always goes on forever ♥ . . . is it right? More salt? More sage? More butter? So taste, and don't worry — we've never measured a thing & it's always delicious! Makes great sandwiches with sliced turkey & cranberry sauce ♥.

SUMMER LOBSTER BOIL
AT THE BEACH

"Summering" on Martha's Vineyard is a tradition with many New England families; the clambake is another tradition. I was new to the East Coast, had never been to a clambake, but I was somehow put in charge of putting together a clambake for fourteen people! And I was just getting over the "I have to cut the oysters in half so I can get used to them" stage! I looked through my (West Coast) cookbooks, but found nothing on a clambake, so I decided to do my own version ~ a lobster boil! It came together so beautifully & was so much fun, that I would do it again in a <u>minute</u> ~ here's what you'll need:

4-wheel-drive truck
2 shovels
wood, lots of it
a large rack from your oven or BBQ
a long board to walk on
large <u>metal</u> bucket or bowl
1 medium-sized metal trash can,
   brand new, with lid
a few rocks, like about 15
fresh water to drink
clam knife, sharp knife
large trash bags
large potholders
paper towels
toilet paper

short-legged beach chairs
flashlight
warm clothes, blankets to sit on
camera
wet washcloths in Tupperware
charcoal
lighter fluid, matches
long tongs
cheesecloth
large heavy paper plates
napkins, forks, cups
butter pots
lobster picks, crackers
beer, wine, soft drinks, coffee
cooler
ghost stories

Menu

Iced littleneck clams on the half shell with horseradish sauce
Steamer clams with melted butter
Live lobsters, 1½ lbs. each   ♥ Condiments :
Roasted corn on the cob   lemon slices
Potato packages (recipe, p. 83)   horseradish sauce
Cheesecake (recipe, p. 115)   1 lb. of butter for melting

To Do Ahead

Make cheesecake, chill, and cover tightly with plastic wrap. Make up one package of potatoes per person. Butter, salt & pepper ears of corn; wrap individually in tin foil ~ 1 or 2 per person. Order lobsters, littlenecks, steamers & ice to be picked up on the way to the beach. Slice lemons, make horseradish sauce (catsup, horse-radish, lemon juice, to taste), put cubes of butter into old saucepan for melting ~ make all beach-proof. Put cold drinks into cooler. Make coffee & fill thermos. Plan for cream & sugar. ♥

Let's Go!

Load up the truck. Put the metal bucket upside-down in the bottom of the trash can (so that lobsters won't go to the bottom). Pick up the ice, fill the cooler & fill the trash can about half-way. Pick up lobsters & clams; put them on top of the ice in the can, cover and go merrily to the beach.

Drive right onto the beach and park for wind break if necessary. Dig a small hole, circle with rocks, fill with charcoal, put grill on top, and light ~ this is for the potatoes & corn. Dig a big hole, fill it with wood, lay the long board across the hole ~ you'll need this board to walk on so that you can get close to the steaming lobsters without falling into the hole. Light the fire. When you're ready, remove the lobsters & clams from the trash ~ can ~ dump out about ½ the ice (use for drinks) but leave the bucket in the can. Put the can on the fire to boil (lid on). Open the icy littleneck clams and serve them raw with horseradish sauce & lemon wedges. When the water is boil ~ ing, melt some butter. Put the steamer clams into the cheesecloth & hang them inside the can until they open. Serve them with melted butter for dipping. Put the potatoes on the grill; cook for ½ hour. Drop lobsters in boiling water; steam for 15 ~ 20 min. Put the corn on the grill for about 8 min. Each person gets a lobster, a package of potatoes, corn on the cob, & a little pot of melted butter ~ pass the picks & lobster crackers. At the end, there's cheesecake & hot coffee. And don't forget those nice wet washcloths you brought along.

The End

We had such a wonderful time ~ we saw the sun drop into the sea, as the moon peeped through the beach grass behind us. One of our company had taken a trip to the library, where he'd boned up on some great ghost stories ~ & we sang all the words to all the songs anyone could remember. The fire was glowing, the moon was big & bright. It was a fabulous evening for all.

EASTER EGG COLORING PARTY

This party has turned out to be an Easter Eve tradition and our celebration of Spring ~ its so much fun to be gathered around a table together talking & painting eggs ~ creativity abounds ♥.

What you'll need :

blown eggs
small paintbrushes
watercolor paints
small jars of water

paper napkins
sharp pencils
3 or 4 jars of fresh
clear nail polish

To blow out the eggs, prick a deep hole in each end of the egg with a needle. Put your mouth over one of the holes & blow hard till the egg comes out ~ it gets easier as the egg starts coming. This should be done before the party starts. Distribute brushes, pencils, etc. around the table ~ use the napkins to blot the brushes. The designs can be drawn (& erased) in pencil. Watercolors dry quick-ly. When completely dry, cover entire egg in clear nail polish. ♥ If your guests sign their eggs you can use them as place cards for Easter Dinner. ♥

"I remember the way we parted,
    The day and the way we met;
You hoped we were both brokenhearted,
    And knew we should both forget.
And the best and the worst of this is
    That neither is most to blame,
If you have forgotten my kisses
    And I have forgotten your name."
                A. C. Swinburne

DESSERTS

CHAMPAGNE COCKTAILS

These are absolutely yummy ~ I like to serve them at a Christmas party, or to my girlfriends at a basket party or wedding shower. ♥ Contrary to one's first reaction, there is little chance of becoming addicted because the aftereffects can be totally devastating. But oh, what a night !♥

Chilled champagne glasses
Good-quality champagne
Sugar cubes
Angostura bitters

Soak the sugar cubes in the bitters. Drop one cube in each chilled champagne glass and fill with champagne. Serve. ♥

"Love is friendship set to music."
Anonymous ♥

CHEESECAKE

My dear friend Laney gave me this receipe about 15 years ago and I still haven't tried one that's better ~ It's a perfect cheesecake and requires no frills.

crust

2½ c. graham cracker crumbs
3/4 c. melted butter

Combine and press into a buttered 9 in. pie plate, building up sides.

filling

1 8 oz. pkg. cream cheese, softened
½ c. sugar
1 Tbsp. lemon juice
½ tsp. vanilla extract
dash salt
2 eggs

Beat softened cream cheese till fluffy. Gradually blend in sugar, lemon juice, vanilla, and salt. Add eggs, one at a time; beat after each. Pour filling into crust. Bake at 325° for 25~30 min., till set.

topping

1½ c. sour cream
3 Tbsp. sugar
3/4 tsp. vanilla

Combine all ingredients and spoon over top of hot cheese~cake. Bake 10 min. longer. Cool ~ Chill several hours.

CRÈME CARAMEL

325° Serves Eight

Light, delicate and elegant ~ also, totally delicious. This is my favorite dessert. ♥ When inverted into serving dish the caramel surrounds the custard like an island. ♥

3 eggs
2 egg yolks
½ c. sugar
2 c. hot milk

1 c. hot cream
1½ tsp. vanilla

♥ ♥ ♥ ♥

¾ c. sugar, melted

Preheat oven to 325° Beat eggs & yolks together, just to blend. Heat milk and cream together. Stir sugar into eggs; slowly add hot milk & cream, stirring constantly. Add vanilla. To make caramel: Put ¾ c. sugar into dry skillet over medium flame. Swirl pan, but don't stir. Cook till deep caramel color. It dries as it cools, so work quickly. Divide the caramel among 8 buttered ramekins & swirl each. Set the dishes into a roasting pan. Pour boiling water into roasting pan to about 1" deep. Pour the custard into ramekins, filling about ¾ full. Put the roasting pan into oven for 45 min. till a knife, inserted in middle, comes out clean. Cool, then chill, covered in refrigerator. To serve, cut tightly around ramekin ~ invert small bowl over ramekin ~ turn both upside-down ~ pudding will slide out. ♥

RICE PUDDING

325° Serves Six

My mother's favorite dessert. I like to serve it
with whipped cream or just plain cream poured over
the top. I think it's a comforting type of dessert,
good in the wintertime, and not unhealthful. ♥

2 c cooked brown rice
3 c whole milk (or whatever you like)
¼ c brown sugar
1 c raisins
½ tsp. mixed cinnamon & nutmeg
3 eggs, beaten

Beat the eggs in a large bowl. Add all the
other ingredients and mix well. Pour into oiled casserole.
Bake at 325° for about one hour, or until set. Serve
it hot or cold. The pudding looks good in an old
fashioned dish or heavy pottery. ♥

CHOCOLATE SHOT COOKIES

325° Makes 2½ dozen

A buttery cookie made for me every year by my Grandma — and I love them. ♥

1 c. butter
1 c. powdered sugar
2 tsp. vanilla
1½ c. unbleached flour
½ tsp. baking soda
1 c. oatmeal
2 bottles chocolate shots

First off, chocolate shots are those little short chocolate pieces sold in plastic containers in the cake decorating section.♥ Cream the butter & sugar till fluffy. Add vanilla, flour, soda & oatmeal, mixing thoroughly. Chill for about 2 hours. Shape into 3 rolls (the width of a cookie) & roll in chocolate shots. Slice 3/8" thick & bake on ungreased cookie sheet for 20~25 min. at 325°. ♥ You can freeze the uncooked rolls & slice off as many as you need (in case of surprise visit by Cookie Monster).♥

"Sweets to the sweet."
♥ Wm. Shakespeare ♥

BANANA FRITTERS

4-5 Servings

This is a very special dessert, crunchy on the outside, soft in the middle.

1 egg
⅓ c. milk
½ c. flour
2 tsp. sugar
½ tsp. baking powder
½ tsp. salt

2 tsp. melted butter
4 bananas
juice of one lemon
2 Tbsp. powdered sugar
cooking oil
sour cream (or ice cream)

Separate the egg & beat the white until stiff. Beat the yolk with milk. Stir in the flour mixed with sugar, baking powder, and salt. Stir in the melted butter. Fold in beaten egg white. Cut the bananas into chunks and squeeze the lemon juice over them. Sprinkle them with the powdered sugar. Dip the banana pieces into the batter and fry in two inches of hot oil. Top with sour cream or ice cream, and serve immediately.

BANANA ICE CREAM

Easy, and healthy. Take frozen banana chunks from your freezer, put in blender with milk to cover, add a tsp. of coffee and a tsp. of vanilla. Blend, serve, yum.

119

APPLE SEASON

Here in New England we celebrate the arrival of Fall in many ways ~ it's an exhilarating time of change signaled at first by a quick drop in temperature, then a gradual turn of the leaves from their Summer greens to the magnificent golds and reds of Fall. It's a time to prepare for the cold to come, to make the garden secure with rototilling and mulch, to finish the last freezing and canning for the Winter supply, to put the pumpkin on the porch and the wreath of dried flowers on the door. Time for cozy dinners of soup and bread and indoor games by a toasty fire. It is also Apple Season 🍎 and is heralded by the many busy roadside stands with their big baskets of juicy apples for sale. I want to give you just a few examples of the different tastes available and some of their uses:

 Granny Smith · Golden Delicious · Cortland · Delicious ·

Tart hard apple ~ use in pies & apple crisp ♥

Sweet, fine-grained, use in salads & for baking ♥

softer sweeter apple ~ use for baked apple ♥

Crispy and juicy~ coat with Caramel for Halloween treats ♥

McIntosh · Jonathan

good eating, wonderful with cheese ♥

Tart and juicy, good for applesauce ♥

APPLE CRISP

375° Serves Six

An old standby with a deliciously crunchy top. Serve it either hot or cold — pour thick cream over or serve with ice cream. ♥

About 4 medium, peeled, sliced, tart apples (Granny Smith)
3/4 c. firmly packed brown sugar
1/2 c. flour
1/2 c. oats
3/4 tsp. cinnamon
3/4 tsp. nutmeg
1/3 c. softened butter

Preheat oven. Butter a square baking pan. Place the apple slices in pan. Mix remaining ingredients and sprinkle over apples. Bake 30 minutes or until apples are tender and topping is golden brown. ♥

"My garden will never make me famous,
I'm a horticultural ignoramus,
I can't tell a stringbean from a soybean,
Or even a girl bean from a boy bean."
Ogden Nash ♥

BLUEBERRY PIE

425°

I feel so lucky because the first summer after I bought my little house on the Vineyard I discovered that it was surrounded by wild blueberry bushes. ♥ And this recipe is the delicious result. I also freeze them so we can have pies in the winter ~ so if you don't have them fresh in your area, frozen ones are fine. ♥

Pie crust dough for two-crust 8" pie (p.)
4 c. blueberries (if frozen, it's not necessary to defrost)
3/4 c. sugar
3½ Tbsp. flour
pinch of salt
squeeze of fresh lemon juice
1 Tbsp. butter

Preheat oven to 425°. Make the pie crust and use half to line an 8" pie plate. In a large bowl mix sugar, flour, and salt. Add blueberries and a squeeze of lemon and mix well. Pour mixture into pie pan & dot evenly with butter. Cover with top crust, trim edges, fold them under & crimp edges. Cut vents in top. Bake for 10 min; lower heat to 325°. Bake 40 min. till top is brown. Serve with vanilla ice cream. ♥

PIE ♥ CRUST

My girlfriend taught me the formula for flaky pie crust & it's never failed me. ♥ For a 9" pie shell (Banana Cream Pie, p. 127) put 1½ c. unbleached flour, ¾ c. shortening & ¾ tsp. salt in a large bowl. Using pastry cutter ⬭, cut through till dough is in pieces the size of peas. Slowly add ice water, mixing with fork, till dough holds together in a ball. Roll out on floured board ~ place in pie pan and crimp edges. If crust is to be pre-baked, prick holes all over the crust, including edges, with fork (to prevent shrinking) ~ place in preheated 475° oven for 10~12 min., till browned. ♥ ♥ ♥ For an 8" two~crust pie (Blueberry, p. 122), use 2 c. flour, 1 c. shortening, 1 tsp. salt & ice water to form ball. ♥ ♥ The formula is this : half as much shortening as flour, ½ tsp. salt per cup of flour & ice water to mix ~ Easy! ♥ ♥ ♥ So make the pretty latticed crust for the top of fruit pies ~ roll out dough, put in pie pan, leaving a 1" overhang ~ pour in filling. Cut remaining rolled-out dough into strips & weave them, in and out over top of pie ~ trim edges. Fold the inch of overhang on bottom crust up & over lattice, building up a high edge. ♥ You can also twist the strips when putting them on. ♥ ♥ For the top crust, as it's usually done, you must cut in vents so air can escape ~ these can be plain or fancy ~ I like to cut out hearts (of course!) or apples ♥ 🍎 ♥ 🍎, whatever you like. ♥ You can also use a little extra dough to form your own little decorations, like leaves 🍃 or flowers ✳ ~ lay them on pie crust & brush with a little milk. ♥ Well, I guess that about covers the subject of pie crust ! ♥ ♥ ♥

CHOCOLATE MOUSSE PIE

Serves Ten

A chocolate dream in a chocolate cookie crust. ♥

Crust:

1½ pkgs. chocolate wafer cookies, crushed
1 Tbsp. fresh coffee granules
6 Tbsp. butter, melted (or more)

Combine all ingredients ~ use additional butter if you think it needs it ~ you'll want it to hold together when you cut it. Reserve about 2 Tbsp. for garnish. Press into 9" pie plate.

Mousse:

1 Tbsp. unflavored gelatin
⅓ c. rum
½ c. sugar
5 eggs, separated
3/4 c. crème de cacao

8 oz. semisweet chocolate
1 Tbsp. instant coffee powder
¼ c. butter, cut into teaspoonfuls
2 c. heavy cream, whipped
1 c. heavy cream, whipped (garnish)

Combine gelatin & rum in a small bowl. Mix well & set aside. Separate eggs ~ reserve whites. Combine sugar & egg yolks in top part of double boiler; beat 3 min. till thickened. Stir in crème de cacao & set over simmering water, beating constantly till mixture is hot & foamy. Remove from heat; add gelatin mixture; beat for 5-6 min. till mixture is cool; set aside. Melt chocolate very slowly in a heavy saucepan. Stir in instant coffee; remove from heat & beat in butter, 1 tsp. at a time. Very slowly, stir the chocolate into egg mixture; beat until mixture is room temperature. Beat reserved egg whites until stiff; fold them into the whipped cream & then fold all into chocolate mixture. Pour into prepared pie plate & refrigerate at least 4 hours. Garnish with additional whipped cream & reserved cookie crumbs. ♥

BERRIES, ROSES & CREAM

Serves Four

As beautiful as it sounds. ♥ A refreshing summer delight. ♥ Any berries will do ~ Raspberries are my favorite, but it's good with strawberries, blueberries or blackberries. ♥

1 c. heavy cream	4 egg yolks
1 c. milk	2½ c. fresh berries or 2 pkg. frozen
1 tsp. rosewater	About 8 fresh pink rose petals, cut
3 Tbsp. sugar	into comfortable pieces & with white
	"heel" at bottom of each petal removed

The rose petals are optional, but they are beautiful floating on top of this dessert & add a light fresh flavor. They should be free of pesticides. The rosewater is available at gourmet food stores. ♥ In the top part of a double boiler heat cream, milk, rosewater & sugar just till warm. Beat egg yolks in a large bowl. Whisk in milk mixture slowly (by the Tbsp. to begin); return to double boiler & cook over low heat, stirring constantly, till thickened (about 10 min.) ~ strain & chill. To serve: use either deep saucers or wine glasses. Put a few berries in the bottom of each dish ~ cover with the chilled custard. Strew more berries over the top and sprinkle on rose petals. Serve. ♥

THREE-LAYER CARROT CAKE

325°

This cake goes together so easily and it has everything: it's very moist, chock-full of nuts and fruit, and it's tall and gorgeous ~ A perfect Birthday Cake. 🕯🕯🕯

4 eggs, well beaten
1 c. packed brown sugar
1 c. white sugar
1½ c. vegetable oil
2 c. unbleached flour
2 tsp. baking soda
2 tsp. baking powder

2 tsp. cinnamon
1½ tsp. nutmeg
3 c. finely grated carrots
1 c. coconut
1 8oz. can crushed pineapple
1 c. golden raisins
1 c. walnuts, coarsely chopped

Preheat oven to 325°. Oil 3 8" cake pans. Set out ½ c. butter, & 1 8oz. pkg. cream cheese to soften (for frosting). Put pineapple in sieve to drain. Beat eggs in large bowl. Add sugars and beat till light & fluffy. Add oil & mix well with whisk. Put in the dry ingredients & beat till smooth. Stir in remaining ingredients & pour batter into oiled layer pans. Bake for 40 minutes or until knife comes out clean when inserted in center of cake. Cool slightly and frost.

Frosting

½ c. butter
8 oz. cream cheese
1 1lb. box powdered sugar
3 tsp. vanilla

Mix together till smooth. Frost between layers & on top. Try toasted coconut for decoration. ♥

BANANA CREAM PIE

This pie is luscious!   Serves Eight

½ c. sugar
6 Tbsp. flour
¼ tsp. salt
2½ c. milk
2 egg yolks
1 Tbsp. butter

½ tsp. vanilla extract
3 ripe bananas
1 baked 9" pie shell (p.123)
½ c. shredded coconut
1½ c. cream, whipped

Mix sugar, flour & salt in the top part of a double boiler. Gradually stir in milk and cook over boiling water ~ stir constantly until thickened. Cover & cook 10 min. longer, stirring occasionally. Beat egg yolks & add to them a small amount of milk mixture. Return mixture to the double boiler & cook for 2 min. over hot, not boiling, water. Stir constantly. Remove from heat ~ stir in butter & extract. Cool. Slice 2 bananas into bottom of pie shell and arrange evenly. Pour cooked mixture over bananas and refrigerate. Spread coconut on a cookie sheet and toast at 350° ~ it burns easily so stir often. Before serving, cover pie with whipped cream, arrange remaining sliced banana around the edge of pie, and put the toasted coconut in the center.

LEMON ICE

Serves Six

Light & icy good. ♥ Serve it in hollowed out lemons or limes. (Cut off a bit of the base in order to set them flat.) Top each with a fresh piece of mint. ♥

3½ c. water
1¼ c. sugar
3/4 c. fresh lemon juice
2 Tbsp. lemon zest
6 fresh mint sprigs

Boil the water in a saucepan; stir in the sugar till dissolved. Remove from heat & cool; add lemon juice & zest. Pour mix-ture into a metal bowl & freeze. When ready to serve, beat the ice till fluffy & scoop into lemon or lime "shells" (or serve in small glass bowls or wine glasses). Top with mint sprigs. ♥

"I would rather sit on a pumpkin and have it all to myself than be crowded on a velvet cushion." ♥ H. Thoreau

KIWI ICE

Light, fresh and very pretty ~ looks especially nice served in sparkly clear glass ~ bowls or sherbet glasses. ♥

4 Kiwi fruit (reserve a perfect slice for each serving.)
5 Tbsp. fresh lemon or lime juice
¼ Tbsp. grated rind
1 c. water
½ c. sugar
½ c. light corn syrup

Pureé fruit, juice and rind in blender. Cook water, sugar and corn syrup until sugar dissolves. Mix it all to~ gether and pour into a shallow pan. Put it in the freezer for 1½ hours. Take it out & beat it till light and fluffy~ Then back to the freezer for at least 2 hours more. Garnish with slices of fresh fruit. Another garnish idea would be fresh mint sprigs or pineapple slices. ♥

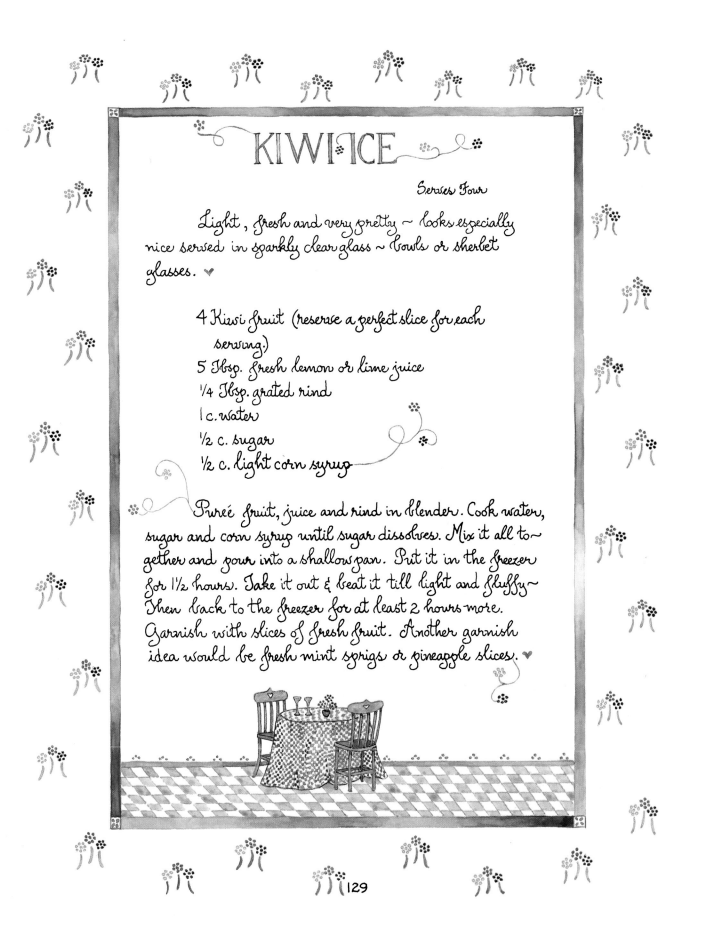

VALENTINE COOKIE

375°   Two Big Cookies

A cute way to celebrate the Day ♥ Fun for you & your children. ♥

½ c. butter

¾ c. packed brown sugar

1 tsp. vanilla

1 egg

1 c. plus 2 Tbsp. unbleached flour

½ tsp. baking soda

½ tsp. salt

1 6 oz. pkg. semi-sweet chocolate chips

½ c. chopped walnuts

Grease two heart-shaped pans. (You can also drop the dough onto greased cookie sheets.) In a large bowl, beat the butter and brown sugar until creamy. Beat in the vanilla and the egg. Mix in flour, soda and salt, then add the chocolate chips and nuts. Divide dough in half and spread in pans, or shape onto cookie sheets. Bake at 375° for 10 to 15 minutes. Cool in pans for 10 minutes, then remove and cool completely. ♥

"The water is wide, I cannot cross o'er.
Neither have I the wings to fly.
Build me a boat that can carry two,
And both shall row, my Love and I."♥

From an American Folk Song

BREAD & BUTTER PUDDING

350°   Serves Eight

A cozy kind of dessert ~ have it in front of the fireplace when the leaves start to fall. ♥

about ½ loaf French bread
6 Tbsp. unsalted butter, softened
4 eggs
3 egg yolks
2 c. milk
1 c. heavy cream
½ c. sugar
2 tsp. vanilla

Preheat oven to 350° Cut crust off of bread & slice ½" thick ~ you'll need 15~20 slices. Butter each slice & overlap them in a buttered 7"×10" baking dish ~ fill dish completely. Combine eggs & yolks in a large mixing bowl & beat them just to blend. In a saucepan combine milk, cream & sugar over medium high heat; bring to simmer to dissolve sugar. Very slowly, whisking constantly, add the hot milk to the eggs. Add the vanilla & pour over prepared bread slices. Place baking dish in a larger pan, then into oven. Pour about 1" hot water into larger pan (so it surrounds baking dish) & bake 45-50 min., till a knife comes out clean. Serve hot or cold, plain, or with whipped cream and/or berries. ♥

CHOCOLATE CREAM PUFFS

375°   Sixteen small puffs

Basic Pastry:
- ♥ ¼ c. butter
- ♥ ½ c. water
- ♥ ½ c. flour
- ♥ 2 eggs, room temp.

Boil the water and butter together in small saucepan. Remove from heat and add flour all at once, beating rapidly till dough leaves the side of the pan and forms a ball. (If it doesn't, put it back on medium heat and keep beating.) Cool for 5 minutes. Add eggs one at a time, beating frantically after each until dough is smooth. Drop small teaspoonfuls on an ungreased cookie sheet 2" apart and bake for about 16 minutes in pre~ heated 375° oven till brown and puffed. Cool. Just before serving, fill with whipped cream by slicing off the very top, & pulling out any wet filaments of dough. Spoon hot chocolate sauce over filled puffs, letting it dribble down the sides. ♥

♥ · ♥ · ♥   Chocolate Sauce   ♥ · ♥ · ♥

Over low flame, heat 3 oz. semi~sweet chocolate & 2 Tbsp. butter, stirring constantly. The sauce will thicken as it cools, so spoon it over puffs rather quickly. ♥

· ♥ · ♥ · ♥

For a charming gift, line a pretty box with large paper doilies, and fill the box with cream puffs, each on its own small round doily. Refrigerate until ready to go. ♥

DEATH BY CHOCOLATE

350° Serves Eight

What a way to go. ♥ Your victims will love you. ♥ A chocolaty ice cream cake roll finished off with a dollop of thick fudgy killer chocolate sauce. ♥

¼ c. cocoa
1¼ c. powdered sugar
5 eggs

1 tsp. vanilla
¼ tsp. salt
1 qt. good vanilla ice cream

Preheat oven to 350°. Sift cocoa & sugar together. Separate the eggs; put the yolks & vanilla in a large bowl & beat very well until thick. In another bowl whisk the egg whites till foamy; add salt & continue beating till soft peaks are formed. Fold the cocoa & sugar into the whites, then gently fold the egg white mixture into the beaten yolks. Thoroughly butter a 10" x 15" cookie sheet & line it with wax paper. Spread the batter evenly in the pan; bake 18~20 min., until knife comes out clean. Sprinkle a clean tea towel with powdered sugar & turn cake out onto it. Remove wax paper & trim off any crispy edges. Roll the cake in the towel from the long end ↑ & let it rest 1-2 min. Unroll & let it rest again for a few min., then roll it up again & allow it to cool completely. Set ice cream out to soften. Unroll the cooled cake; spread evenly with ice cream & roll it back up (without the tea towel). Dust the top with powdered sugar. Keep it in the freezer till ready to serve. When ready, cut the cake & serve it with the hot chocolate sauce on the side. ♥

Killer Chocolate Sauce

3 Tbsp. unsalted butter
4 oz unsweetened chocolate
2/3 c. boiling water

1½ c. sugar
7 Tbsp. corn syrup
1 tsp. vanilla

Melt the butter & chocolate in a heavy saucepan over low heat; add boiling water & stir well. Mix in the sugar & corn syrup ~till sauce is smooth. Boil the sauce, without stirring, for 10 min.; remove from heat; cool 20 min., then add the vanilla. Spoon the sauce over the ice cream cake and serve. ♥

WINTER WARMERS
Dessert Chocolate

4 servings in mugs ♥   10 servings in demitasse ♥

Rich delicious hot chocolate ~ a very special ending to a meal.

4 oz. semi~sweet chocolate   1 c. heavy cream, whipped

⅓ c. sugar   Peppermint Schnapps (opt.)

1¼ c. boiling water   Fresh coffee grains (opt.)

4 c. very hot milk   cocoa powder (opt.)

1 tsp. vanilla   cinnamon stick swizzles (opt.)

Melt the chocolate in double boiler ~ stir in the sugar, then slowly add boiling water, whisking well. Stir in the very hot milk. Simmer about 7~8 min. Beat very well until frothy; stir in vanilla. ♥ If using demi-tasse, put about 1 Tbsp. Peppermint Schnapps in each cup. Fill with hot chocolate ~ add a dollop of whipped cream & a sprinkle of either coffee grains or cocoa powder & serve. ♥ If using mugs, put a shot of Schnapps in each mug; fill with chocolate; top with whipped cream. Sprinkle on cocoa or coffee grains ~ add a cinnamon stick to each mug & serve. ♥

Hot Buttered Rum

Makes 12 servings

½ c. brown sugar   3 c. dark rum

½ c. butter   ♥ Cream all ingredients (except rum)

¼ tsp. each: cinnamon,   together & beat well. Put ¼ c. rum

  cloves & nutmeg   into each cup ~ add 2 tsp. butter

1 Tbsp. lemon zest   mixture, fill with boiling water;
                              stir well & serve. ♥

SUMMER COOLERS

Agua de Limón

2 10oz. servings

The most refreshing drink in the world! The ice must be well crushed & it should be served with straws ♥. When I was in Mexico, they kept drawers full of limes for this wonderful purpose ♥.

2 iced glasses   crushed ice
juice of 5 or 6 fresh limes   fresh water
3~4 Tbsp. sugar   2 fresh mint sprigs (opt.)

Divide the juice evenly between the two iced glasses. Put 1½ Tbsp. sugar into each glass & stir until sugar dissolves. Fill each glass with crushed ice & then water. Stir very well so drink is icy cold. You might need more sugar so taste & decide for yourself. ♥ ♥ Garnish with fresh mint, pop in some straws & serve ♥.

Kahlúa Shake

2 10 oz. servings

Frothy & fun. ♥ Perfect after summer sports. ♥

2 oz. Kahlúa   3 scoops vanilla ice cream
2 oz. vodka   crushed ice
1 c. milk   large straws

Put Kahlúa, vodka, milk & ice cream into blender. Blend on high speed for about 35 seconds. Fill 10 oz. glasses half way with crushed ice; pour in Kahlúa mixture; stir well. Add straws & serve. ♥

"Stands the church clock at ten to three?
And is there honey still for tea?"
Rupert Brooke

BREAKFAST

"You have to eat oatmeal or you'll
dry up. Anybody knows that."
Eloise ♥ Kay Thompson ♥

137

♥·· ♥ BREAKFAST ♥···♥

Breakfast! My favorite meal ~ you can be so creative. I think of bowls of sparkling berries and fresh cream, baskets of ♫ Popovers and Croissants ♪ with little pots of jams and jellies, steaming coffee and freshly squeezed orange juice, thick country bacon, hot maple syrup, pancakes and French toast ~ even the nutty flavor of Irish Oatmeal with brown sugar and cream. ♥ Breakfast is the place I splurge with calories, then I spend the rest of the day getting ♪ them off! I love to use my prettiest table settings ~ crocheted placemats with lace-edged napkins and old hammered silver. And whether you are inside in front of a fire, candles burning brightly on a wintery day ~ or outside on a patio enjoying the morning sun ~ whether you are having a group of friends and family, ♫ a quiet little brunch for two, or an even quieter little brunch just for yourself ♥, breakfast can set the mood and pace of the whole day.

♪ And Sunday is my day. ♥ Sometimes I think we get caught up in the hectic happenings of the weeks and months and ♫ we forget to take time out to relax. So one snowy Sunday I decided to do things differently ~ now ♪ it's gotten to be a sort of ritual! This is what I do: at around 8:30 am. I pull myself from my warm cocoon, fluff up the pillows and blankets and put some classical music on the stereo. ♥ Then I'm off to the kitchen, where I very calmly (so as not to wake myself up too much!) prepare my breakfast, ♪ something extra nice ~ last week I had fresh pineapple slices wrapped in bacon and broiled, a warm croissant, hot chocolate with marshmallows & orange juice. I put ♪ it all on a tray with a cloth napkin, my book-of-the-moment and the "Travel" section of the Boston Globe and take it back to bed with me. There I ♪ ♪ spend the next 2 hours reading, eating and dreaming ♥ while the snowflakes swirl through the treetops outside my bedroom

♥ ♥ ♥ ♥ ♥

window. ♪ The inspiring music of Bach or Vivaldi adds an exquisite elegance to the otherwise unruly scene, and I am in heaven. ♡ I found time to get in touch with myself and my life ♪ and I think this just might be a necessity! Please try it for yourself, and someone you love. ♡

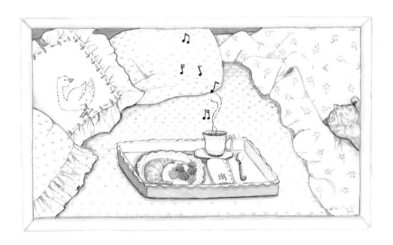

"There is a pleasure in the pathless woods,
    There is rapture on the lonely shore,
        There is society, where none intrudes,
            By the deep Sea, and Music in its roar:
                I love not Man the less, but Nature more."
                                Lord Byron

BEST BISCUITS

425° Makes about 14

Hot, flaky, melt-in-your-mouth biscuits ~ for breakfast! Best served with honey butter: a mixture of softened butter and honey to taste. ♥ Don't forget these for your Sunday chicken dinners. ♥ And one more idea: chop fresh strawberries & heat them with a tiny bit of sugar to taste. Pour the berries over hot, split biscuits ~ finish with a big dollop of sweetened whipped cream. ♥

2 c. unbleached flour
1 Tbsp. baking powder
1¼ tsp. salt

2½ tsp. sugar
1½ c. heavy cream
4 Tbsp. melted butter

Preheat oven to 425°. Put flour, baking powder, salt & sugar into mixing bowl ~ stir with fork. Slowly add 1 to 1½ c. cream, stirring constantly, just until dough comes together. Place dough on floured board & knead for 1 minute. Pat dough flat to about ¾" thick. Cut with round 2" cookie cutter & brush both sides with melted butter. Place the buttered biscuits 1" apart on ungreased cookie sheet. Bake 15 ~ 18 min., till browned. Wrap them in a napkin & serve them in a basket. ♥

APPLESAUCE

Makes 4 cups

Make your own applesauce, and it won't be the smoothed~out kind you get at the market. I like to serve it hot at breakfast with Popovers (p.149) or German Pancake (p.147) or Cottage Cheese Pancakes (p.148). Also very good with Veal Birds (p.97). I make it and put it up in jars and give it away at Christmastime. ♥

4 med. tart apples, peeled, cored & quartered
1 c. water
½ c. brown sugar
¼ tsp. cinnamon
⅛ tsp. nutmeg
1 Tbsp. butter
¾ c. chopped walnuts (opt.)
½ c. raisins, golden kind (opt.)
⅓ c. coconut (opt.)

Put the apples & water in a pot and heat over medium heat until boiling. Reduce to simmer and stir occasionally for 5 to 10 minutes until apples are tender. Add all the other ingredients and heat through until raisins are plumped. ♥

♥ ♥ ♥ ♥ ♥ ♥ ♥

CORNMEAL MUFFINS

375° Makes 1 dozen

For this recipe I love to use my cast iron muffin pans that symbolize the four seasons. Folklore says that the heart shape is for spring, the round cup for the summer sun, the scalloped cup for the fall foliage and the star stands for the winter sky. The cups are shallow so the muffins come out extra crisp and light. When using this type of pan, fill the cups full, but when using a regular muffin pan, only fill it 2/3 full. ♥

½ c. yellow cornmeal
½ c. unbleached flour
2 tsp. baking powder
1½ tsp. sugar
1 tsp. salt

½ tsp. cinnamon
1 egg
3/4 c. milk
2 Tbsp. melted butter
Honey butter

Preheat oven to 375° Sift all dry ingredients into a bowl. Mix liquids together, then combine with dry ingredients. Pour batter into well~buttered muffin pans and bake for 20 min. until lightly browned. Serve with honey butter: cream softened butter with honey to taste. ♥

CRISPY POTATO PANCAKES

Serves Six

Brown and crispy, these are great with sausages and homemade applesauce (p.141) for breakfast. ♥

4 large russet potatoes
1 egg, beaten
1½ Tbsp. flour
2 Tbsp. cream
salt & pepper to taste
oil for frying

Peel the potatoes and grate them. Put them in a large tea towel & twist to remove moisture. Immediately put the potatoes into a bowl with beaten egg, flour, cream, and salt & pepper. (The potatoes will turn brown if not cooked immediately after grating.) Mix well. Heat oil in large skillet. Put a couple of spoonfuls into the hot oil and mash with spatula to form a pancake. Cook them over moderate heat till browned on both sides. Put them in a warm oven till they're all cooked. Serve hot. ♥

STRAWBERRIES IN THE SUN

Makes Two Pints

This is a very different, very delicious way to make Strawberry
Preserves ~ the berries stay almost whole. ♥ If you're lucky enough
to have a Berry Garden, ♥ this would be a good way to use the
surplus ~ also makes a lovely gift for your friends. ♥

3 pounds nice whole
  berries, well~ripened
  but not bruised
1½ pounds sugar
½ c. water

Wash, hull and dry the berries. Mix the sugar & water together
in a large heavy saucepan. Place on heat & bring to a boil. Keep
boiling for 5 minutes, then add the strawberries to the syrup.
Bring back to the boil & cook for 5 more minutes. Pour the mix~
ture into a large roasting pan, spreading it no thicker than
2 inches. This is the fun part: ♥ run around your house &
find a window screen you can spare for four days. Rinse it
off and dry it ~ then cover the roasting pan with it, and
take the berries out in the sun for 4 days, bringing them
in at night. The liquid will slowly evaporate; the berries
will become swollen with the heavy syrup. You can then ladle
the preserves into hot, sterilized jars and seal. It's the Berries! ♥

HOMEMADE DONUTS

Makes about 20

Fresh, hot~from~the~oven donuts ~ they make you an instant hero! Make the dough the day before for more relaxed donut making. They can also be frozen, then baked, unthawed, at 350° for 15min.

1 donut cutter, 2¾" diameter
1 deep~fry thermometer
2 Tbsp. warm water
1 pkg. dry yeast
½ c. sugar

1 egg, room temp.
2 Tbsp. melted butter
1 c. warm milk
3½ c. unbleached flour
½ tsp. salt

Pour the warm water over the yeast in a medium-sized mixing bowl. Stir; add sugar, mixing well. Let stand for 15 min. Stir in egg, then the butter, milk, flour & salt. Mix until dough becomes elastic. Brush additional melted butter lightly over top of dough & cover with waxed paper. Drape tea-towel over top of bowl and put it in a warm place to rise for 2 hours. Then refrigerate over night (not necessary, but chilling the dough will make it easier to roll out). When ready, punch down in the bowl then turn it out on a heavily floured board. Take half the dough & roll to ½" thick; cut with floured donut cutter; put them on well~buttered waxed paper on cookie sheet. Do other half of dough ~ put cookie sheet in a warm place till donuts double in size, about 1 hour. Heat 4" of oil for deep frying ~ 365° on thermometer. Regulate heat to keep temp. steady. Gently remove donuts with spatula into hot oil, turning once, till golden. Drain them on paper towels. While still warm cover with: Granulated Sugar or

Chocolate   or   Glaze

Melt 3oz. semi~sweet choco~ late & 3oz. butter. Stir in ¾ c. confectioners sugar. Frost ♥.

Mix together 1 c. confectioners sugar, 2 Tbsp. fresh lemon juice & 1 Tbsp. honey. Glaze ♥.

145

COTTAGE CHEESE PANCAKES

Makes 8 Pancakes

These pancakes are healthier, have more texture, & taste better than normal pancakes. Serve them with hot Applesauce (p.141) and Banana Fritters with ice cream (p. 119) for a warming winter breakfast feast. ♥

1 c. cottage cheese, drained	2 Tbsp. melted butter
3 eggs	¼ tsp. cinnamon
¼ c. flour	¼ tsp. salt

Squeeze the cottage cheese dry in a piece of cheesecloth. Beat the eggs in a mixing bowl; add the cottage cheese & all other ingredients — mix just to blend. Drop by large spoonfuls into buttered & oiled moderately hot skillet. Cook fairly slowly until brown on both sides. Keep them warm in a 200° oven till all are done. Serve with heated Vermont maple syrup. ♥

"The wind was blowing, but not too hard, and everyone was so happy and gay for it was only twenty degrees below zero and the sun shone."
Laura Ingalls Wilder ♥

POPOVERS

400° Makes 12

These will pop up and over the top of the muffin pan ~ Serve them with marmalade and jam. ♥

3 eggs
1½ c. milk
1 Tbsp. melted butter
1 tsp. salt
1½ c. unbleached flour

Butter 12 cups in muffin pans. Beat all ingredients together until smooth. Fill muffin pans ⅔ full. Bake at 400° for 45 minutes. Take them out and slit the tops ~ return to the oven for 5~10 minutes. Serve them in a large basket wrapped in a pretty cloth. ♥

BREAKFAST CRÊPES

Makes 12 crêpes

Crêpes are very easy & kind of fun to make. ♥ I usually triple this recipe & stack them with waxed paper in between & then freeze them. There are lots of ways to use them. ♥

2 eggs, beaten well
1 c. milk
1 c. unbleached flour

1½ Tbsp. butter, melted
½ tsp. vanilla (opt.)
pinch of salt

Add milk to beaten eggs — whisk in all other ingredients; mix till smooth. Lightly oil a 7" skillet (Teflon works great); heat pan till moderately hot. Using a small measuring cup, pour about 3 Tbsp. batter into pan & quickly swirl to coat the bottom (like a very thin pancake). Brown lightly & turn to cook other side. Remove to plate. Finish all & fill with:

Ricotta Filling

Serves Six   (2 crêpes each)

Mix together 1 lb. Ricotta cheese, 1 beaten egg, 3 Tbsp. powdered sugar & 2 tsp. lemon zest. Roll into crêpes, dust with powdered sugar & sprinkle over chopped fresh strawberries — serve. ♥ ♥ Apple topping for Ricotta-filled crêpes: Put peeled chopped apples in skillet with a little butter. Add brown sugar, chopped walnuts, & a little cinnamon to taste — cook till apples soften & pour over filled crêpes. ♥ Crêpes Chantilly: Mix 1 thinly sliced banana with 1 c. whipped cream, 2 Tbsp. powdered sugar & ½ tsp. vanilla. Fill crêpes; top with more sliced banana; sprinkle on some toasted almonds & serve. ♥

BEER BREAD

350° Makes 1 loaf

Imagine . . . fresh bread in a matter of minutes! Good bread too & healthy. ♥ Makes delicious toast. ♥

1 12 oz. can of beer
¼ c. maple syrup
3 Tbsp. caraway seeds
2 c. whole wheat flour
1 c. unbleached flour
4 Tbsp. baking powder
1 tsp. salt

Preheat oven to 350°. Use beer containing no preservatives (Miller). In a small saucepan warm up the beer, maple syrup & caraway seeds. Mix together remaining ingredients, pour warm liquid into flour mixture & mix it up quickly. Pour batter into well-buttered loaf pan. Bake 30 min. ♥ You can also use buttered muffin tins for crusty rolls. Bake for 15 min. ♥

" He drew a circle that shut me out—
 Heretic, rebel, a thing to flout.
 But Love and I had the wit to win:
 We drew a circle that took him in."
 ♥ Edwin Markham ♥

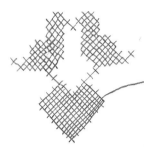

EGGS IN TOMATOES

350° Serves Six

Cooked tomatoes for breakfast is an English tradition ♥.
Serve these with Best Biscuits (p. 140) & soft potato pancakes
(form mashed potatoes into patties; dip in flour; fry in butter).

3 large tomatoes
salt
6 eggs
thyme leaves
6 tsp. butter

6 Tbsp. heavy cream
6 Tbsp. jack cheese, grated
3 Tbsp. fine bread crumbs
2 Tbsp. parsley, minced
freshly ground pepper

Preheat oven to 350°. Cut the tomatoes in half; hollow them
out, salt the insides & invert to drain for about 15 min.
(Make Best Biscuits ♥) Put about 2 Tbsp. water in baking
dish & bake tomato shells for 8 min. Remove from oven &
allow to cool slightly. Drop an egg into each tomato half;
sprinkle each with a generous pinch of thyme; add a tsp.
of butter & a Tbsp. of cream to each. Mix the cheese,
bread crumbs, parsley & pepper, to taste; divide the mixture evenly over tomatoes & bake for 16~18 min. Serve ♥.

BREAKFAST · IDEAS

♥ The "Come as you are" party: This was something my parents did during the summers when I was a child & I remember them because they were so much fun. We have wonderful photos of these parties — adults & children all in their pajamas out in our backyard playing croquet, eating a barbecued breakfast, enjoying the early morning sunshine ~ a (planned) spur-of-the-moment party. Secrecy is the key to success. Plan the party ~ make a few loose groundrules about "acceptable party clothes" & simply go to your guests' homes at 7 a.m. on a warm Saturday morning & start rounding them up. After the shock wears off, you'll have a memorable party. ♥

♥ Breakfast hors d'oeuvres: wrap fresh pineapple slices in half-cooked bacon ~ before serving, put them under the broiler to finish the bacon. ♥ Hot Cornmeal Muffins (p. 142) served with honey butter. ♥ Fill triangles of Phyllo with a mixture of Ricotta cheese, powdered sugar & lemon zest. Fry quickly in hot butter & oil ~ Sift over a bit more powdered sugar & serve. ♥ Dip large cold strawberries in Chocolate Sauce (p. 132) ~ or serve fresh strawberries with a bowl of sweetened whipped cream for dipping. ♥ Make French toast out of cinnamon swirl bread ~ put orange marmalade between the slices; cut into bite-sized pieces. Serve them with yogurt mixed with brown sugar for dipping. ♥ Put watermelon balls on toothpicks; mix sour cream & brown sugar for dipping. ♥

153

"Everyone has, inside himself . . .
what shall I call it? A piece
of good news! Everyone is . . .
a very great, very important
character."

Ugo Betti

"FRIENDS ~

They are kind
to each other's
HOPES.

They cherish
each other's
DREAMS."

Thoreau

My heartfelt thanks & gratitude for the special encouragement from Stan Hart, Jane Bay & Cliff Branch. ♥ And to my new friend, Robin Ledoux ~ who is talented, committed & inspiring ~ thank you! ♥ Special thanks to Sandy Haeger, who took the time to help me.

"A" is for Apple(s) . . .

INDEX

"The sweetest flower that blows,
I give you as we part.
For you it is a rose
For me it is my heart."

Frederick Peterson

VINEYARD SEASONS

No matter what
the seasons be
My books bring
sunshine home to me.

"THEREFORE ALL
SEASONS
SHALL BE SWEET
TO THEE..."

♥ Samuel Taylor Coleridge

"One morning we ran into a
neighbor at the store and she
asked brightly,
   'What was it at your house?'
'Fourteen below,' we replied.
Her face fell. 'We had minus
twelve,' she said, and you
could see that her day was ruined."

♥ Richard Ketchum

A TIME TO EVERY PURPOSE UNDER HEAVEN

VINEYARD SEASONS

MORE FROM THE HEART OF THE HOME

BY SUSAN BRANCH

LITTLE, BROWN AND COMPANY

BOSTON   TORONTO

FIRST EDITION

Library of Congress Cataloging-in-Publication Data
Branch, Susan.
   Vineyard seasons.

   Includes index.
   1. Cookery.   2. Entertaining.   I. Title.
   TX715.B8176   1988   641.5   88-9984
   ISBN 0-316-10632-1

♡ Excerpt from "Symptom Recital" in The Portable Dorothy Parker. Copyright 1926, 1955 by Dorothy Parker. By permission of Viking Penguin, Inc. and Gerald Duckworth.
♥ Excerpt from Grapefruit by Yoko Ono. Copyright © 1964, 1970 by Yoko Ono. Reprinted by permission of Simon and Schuster, Inc. and Peter Owen Ltd., London.
♡ Excerpt from "The Look" in Collected Poems by Sara Teasdale. Copyright 1915 by Macmillan Publishing Company, renewed 1943 by Mamie T. Wheless. Reprinted by permission of Macmillan Publishing Company.

PRINTED IN THE UNITED STATES OF AMERICA

Sue

Jim

Steve

FOR MOM

This is a surprise for my mother: these little pictures of her fabulous children & this dedication.

Because of my creative mother I became proficient at many wonderful things: I can twirl the baton & I'm a wicked jacks player (tho' never as wicked as she!). I know the very best lagger for hopscotch & all the best hide-& go-seek places on Claire Avenue. I speak "Arf & Arfy" fluently, know games to play on babies' faces & can sing the words to wonderful songs that no one else ever heard of. She ordered "Rock Around the Clock" from American Bandstand & taught us how to dance, tightened my roller skates with a key before I went out & helped us put on a circus complete with "Man Eating Tigers" (one of my brothers sitting behind a curtain eating animal crackers).

Her patience was never-ending, her heart is gold & I love her, my mom, Patricia Louise Stewart. ♥

Chuck

Brad

Paula

Mary

Shelly

P.S. I want no flak from you kids about these pictures...I did my best! ♥

CONTENTS

"A little house — a house of my own —
Out of the wind's and the rain's way."
💜 Padraic Colum

APPETIZERS

"It is extraordinary how music sends one
back into memories of the past ⌒ and it
is the same with smells."

George Sand ♥

STEAK TARTARE
Makes 2 cups

The beef should be partially frozen when ground, so it will be icy cold when served. It's good to set the serving dish in a bowl of ice. ♥

1 lb. beef tenderloin, partially frozen
3 Tbsp. minced onion
2 Tbsp. minced parsley
6 shakes Tabasco sauce
1½ tsp. Worcestershire sauce
4 tsp. capers
freshly ground black pepper, to taste
½ tsp. ruby port
pumpernickel cocktail bread
sweet butter

Cut beef into 1" cubes ~ grind in food processor 6 ~ 8 seconds. Combine onion, parsley, Tabasco, Worcestershire, capers, pepper & port; then stir in beef. Spread pumpernickel slices with sweet butter and serve alongside the steak tartare. ♥

"He that is of a merry heart hath
a continual feast."
♥ Proverbs 15:15

SALMON-STUFFED PUMPERNICKEL

Great for a buffet. ♥

½ lb. smoked salmon
1 8-oz. pkg cream cheese
3 green onions
2 tsp. Worcestershire
2 tbsp. fresh lemon juice
½ c. milk

½ tsp. Tabasco
¼ c. capers, drained
1 whole, round loaf
   pumpernickel
1 pkg. pumpernickel
   cocktail bread

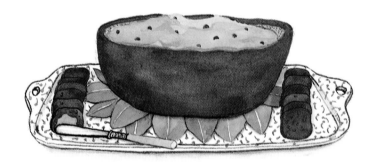

Put first 7 ingredients into food processor & blend till smooth. Stir in capers. Cover & refrigerate until ready to serve. Cut the top off the round loaf of pumpernickel bread & hollow it out. Fill with salmon mixture & serve with cocktail bread. ♥

"... our life is what our thoughts make it."
   ♥ Marcus Aurelius

"GIRL TALK" HORS D'OEUVRE

350° Serves Two

Get your best friend and a good bottle of red wine. You'll also need 2 large heads of fresh garlic, some good olive oil, 2 small logs of Montrachet cheese, some thyme, about ½ loaf of fresh French bread, ½ c. fresh bread~ crumbs & ripe pears, crisp juicy apples, or seedless grapes.

This takes 1 hour from start to finish & it's fun to do together. Don't peel the garlic, leave it whole; just cut off the very tips ♥ (as you would trim an artichoke) so that when you pour the oil over, it will get into the cloves of garlic. Put the garlic heads into a small baking dish & pour olive oil over the tops to a depth of about ½". Cover dish & place in 350° oven for 1 hour. Meanwhile place cheese in oven~ proof dish, brush with olive oil, sprinkle on lots of thyme; pat on breadcrumbs to cover. Place dish, uncovered, into oven for last 30 minutes of cooking time. Now put equal parts of butter & olive oil in a large frying pan (about 2 Tbsp. each); add 2 minced cloves garlic. Slice the bread into ½" slices. Fry the slices till toasty brown on both sides. When the hour is up remove the garlic heads from the oil & place on serving dish along with cheese & toast~ ed bread. Serve with cold pear slices, apples or grapes.

The garlic becomes very mellow & spreadable after cooking ~ just slip the cloves out of their skins & spread on toast with the hot cheese ~ yum. A good dose of wonderful conversation is the last ingredient for a special time. ♥

FONDUE

A fondue is best served as an hors d'oeuvre at a party rather than as a main dish or dessert. It must be kept warm in a chafing dish & I think it adds nice "texture" to the table. ♥

Chocolate   2 cups

I always serve something sweet for balance. ♥

12 oz. semi-sweet chocolate
2/3 c. heavy cream
2 Tbsp. Triple Sec
fruit & cake

Heat the chocolate & cream, stirring over low heat till chocolate melts. Stir in Triple Sec. Keep warm over _very_ low flame; stir occasionally & serve with dipping pieces of bananas, pears, angel food cake, strawberries, pineapple, cherries & apples. ♥

Cheese   2 Cups

This is sort of the traditional cheese fondue ~ I sometimes use the cheese sauce in Welsh Rabbit (p. 116) for a change. ♥

1 clove garlic	2 tsp. cornstarch
1 c. dry white wine	3 Tbsp. kirsch
8-oz. Gruyère, grated	salt, fresh pepper
8-oz. Jarlsberg, grated	sprinkle of nutmeg
	French-bread pieces

Rub a heavy pot with garlic, leaving shreds in pot. Add wine, bring to boil. Add cheeses, lower heat & stir till melted. Dissolve cornstarch in kirsch, add to cheese. Salt & pepper to taste; sprinkle over nutmeg. Keep over _very low_ flame. Serve with bread chunks for dipping, or vegetable pieces. Thin with hot wine if necessary. ♥

YAM CHIPS

Slightly sweet & a nice change. ♥
   3 large yams
   oil for frying
   salt

Peel yams & slice crosswise as thinly as possible. Soak the slices in a big bowl filled with ice & water ½ hr. Drain & thoroughly dry with paper towels. Heat ½" oil in skillet till almost smoking. Fry chips several at a time (don't crowd them) till golden, turning once. Drain on paper towels, blotting to remove excess oil. Salt to taste & serve. ♥

ROASTED FRENCH FRIES

Broiled with a delicious crunch of Parmesan cheese. ♥
   3 large baking potatoes
   ¼ c. melted butter
   Parmesan cheese (grated)
   salt

Don't peel, but cut potatoes into long thin strips. Soak in ice water 1 hour; drain & plunge into boiling water. Cook 5 min. till almost tender. Drain, rinse in cold water, thoroughly pat dry. Preheat broiler. Arrange potatoes on cookie sheet. Brush with melted butter, sprinkle with cheese & salt. Broil about 10 min. till brown & crunchy. Serve. ♥

STUFFED GRAPE LEAVES
Makes about 30

This island wasn't named Martha's Vineyard for no reason—wild grapevines are abundant ♥. In the winter we gather the vines to twist & weave into wreaths & in the summer we choose the tenderest leaves to stuff & eat—delicious! (The beautiful green leaves also look wonderful as liners for summer hors d'oeuvre platters, or underneath butter pats on bread plates.) ♥

To gather fresh leaves: of course they must be unsprayed; wild or domestic; clean, whole, flexible & of med. size. Gather & stack them & then, using tongs, dip the stacks in 2 qts. boiling water mixed with 4 tsp. pickling salt for 30 seconds. Drain; gently press out excess moisture. Wrap & freeze or go right on with the recipe. ♥

40 grape leaves, fresh or preserved	1 tsp. cinnamon
1 sm. onion, minced	6 lg. dried prunes, minced
1/3 c. pecans, finely chopped	1/4 c. parsley, minced
3 Tbsp. olive oil	2 Tbsp. fresh lemon juice
1½ c. cooked brown rice	freshly ground pepper

If using preserved leaves, thoroughly rinse in cold water; remove any woody stems. Sauté onion & pecans in oil till onion is tender. Add rice, cinnamon, prunes, parsley, lemon juice, & pepper to taste. Line a heavy pot with grape leaves. On the rest of the leaves put 1 tsp. mixture in the center of each, vein side up. Turn in top of leaf, then sides; roll up. Place in pot, add 1½ c. water. Put a plate on top of them so they stay submerged. Cover the pot & simmer 30 min. Serve cool but not cold. ♥

15

I LOVE NEW YORK

The love of my life has an Aunt Peggy, the youngest 82-year-old I've ever met, who lives in a wonderful old building in New York. We walked over for cocktails on a chilly night in late winter~ it was the beginning of a memorable evening that included wonderful stories of sailing on the <u>Queen Elizabeth</u>, of Fred Astaire on stage in 1932, of music by Bobby Short & of watching a beautiful face remember things that could only live in my imagination. It was a step back in time & it began with this little hors d'oeuvre that Peggy had whipped up before our arrival. It just seemed so old-fashioned & New Yorkish to me. It is very simple to prepare & the ingredients can always be kept on hand. You'll need: hard-boiled egg yolks, mayonnaise, capers, minced anchovies, freshly ground pepper & bite-sized toast. Mash the yolks & mix with mayonnaise to make a light paste; add the rest of ingredients to taste & pile on toast. ♥ Pull the curtains, put on some old music, serve your favorite cocktails & dream about what it must have been like to sail to Europe a long time ago. ♥

MONTRACHET WON TONS
Makes 36

Hot, melted Montrachet inside crisp fried wonton skins, & the best thing is they can be cooked & frozen so at "the party" all you have to do is reheat them. ♥

6 oz. cream cheese, softened
2 egg yolks
2 Tbsp. sour cream
2/3 c. Montrachet
2 tsp. thyme

6 Tbsp. shredded Parmesan
2 green onions, minced
salt & pepper
36 wonton wrappers
cornstarch & water to seal

oil for frying

Blend cream cheese, yolks, sour cream, Montrachet, thyme & Parmesan. Stir in onions & salt & pepper to taste. Mix together 1 Tbsp. cornstarch with 1 c. hot water. Wonton wrappers dry out quickly so keep them (finished & unfinished) under a damp cloth. Lay out wonton, dip finger in cornstarch water & brush 4 edges of wonton. Put 1 tsp. filling in center & fold to make a triangle, pressing edges to seal. Bring corners up together, overlap slightly, moisten & pinch together. Fry in ¼ in. hot oil till browned on all sides. Serve, or cool & freeze. To reheat: do not thaw. Place on cookie sheet & bake in 350° oven for 15 minutes. ♥

Sun-Dried Tomato Bites

425° Makes 24

Watch out for these; they go fast because they are totally irresistible. ♥

¼ c. olive oil
2 cloves garlic, mashed
1 French-bread baguette
12 oz. Montrachet cheese
¼ c. sour cream
½ tsp. each thyme & rosemary
9 sun-dried tomatoes, coarsely chopped
freshly ground black pepper

Preheat oven to 425°. Crush garlic into olive oil. Thinly slice baguette. Mash Montrachet with enough sour cream to make it spreadable. Add the thyme & rosemary. Chop the tomatoes. Lay the sliced bread on a cookie sheet & brush with garlic oil (one side only). Bake till lightly toasted. Remove from oven & turn them all over. Put a thick layer of the cheese mixture on each, sprinkle on sun-dried tomatoes, grind pepper over all, and bake 3 min., till cheese is melted. Serve. ♥ Sometimes I serve these with the salad for the first course at dinner. ♥

"Basically my wife was immature. I'd be
   at home in the bath and she'd come in
   and sink my boats." ♥ Woody Allen

HOW TO
SUN-DRY TOMATOES

This is a summer occupation, to do when the sun is hot and the tomatoes ripe and flavorful. There is really nothing to it, yet I have paid as much as $6 for a tiny little jar of them. And they're sooo good! On page 106 you'll find a wonderful recipe for a Sun-Dried Tomato Pesto; I've used them in the delicious Pizza on page 115, & in the appetizer on page 18. They keep indefinitely, which makes them a perfect Christmas gift or a way to bring sunshine to a wintery day.

Use the extra-flavorful Italian tomatoes, plum or Roma. Cover an oven rack with cheesecloth. Cut the tomatoes in half lengthwise & lay them, cut side up, on the cheesecloth. Cover with another piece of cheesecloth. Take them outside & keep them in full sun for 2-3 days, bringing them in at night. They're perfect when dry & shriveled but flexible, not brittle. Pack them sort of loosely in jars & pour over good virgin olive oil to cover. You can add fresh basil leaves or sprigs of rosemary if you like. Cover tightly & keep at room temperature. As I said, they'll keep forever; as long as the oil tastes good & fresh, they're fine ♥.

"Ten measures of speech descended on the world; women took nine and men one." ♥ Babylonian Talmud

SPINACH BALLS ♥

300° Makes 50

Wonderful because they can be made ahead & frozen—just bake as many as you need at a time. You can double & triple this recipe ♥.

2 pkg. frozen chopped spinach
4 beaten eggs
2 c. herb stuffing (packaged)
½ c. Parmesan cheese
1 garlic clove, minced

1 chopped onion
1½ tsp. thyme
3/4 c. butter, melted
salt & pepper

Cook spinach (according to pkg.); drain & squeeze dry. Mix together all ingredients. Chill for 2 hours. Roll into 1" balls. Freeze on cookie sheet. When frozen, store in plastic bags till needed. Thaw before baking. Bake at 300° for 30 minutes. ♥

PESTO "RAVIOLI"
WITH WINE SAUCE

Makes 24

This makes an elegant beginning to an Italian dinner. ♥

½ c. ricotta
2 Tbsp. basil pesto ★
24 won ton wrappers
2 Tbsp. butter
2 Tbsp. olive oil
2 cloves garlic, minced

⅓ c. white wine
2 Tbsp. parsley, minced
1 tsp. lemon juice
freshly ground pepper
Parmesan cheese
¼ c. pine nuts, toasted

Mix together ricotta & pesto (there's a recipe for pesto on p. 79 of _Heart of the Home_). One at a time, put a rounded tsp. of pesto mixture in the center of won ton wrapper. Dip your finger in a glass of water & moisten edges. Fold diagonally; press edges together. Keep finished ones under damp cloth. When all are done, place as many as can fit, without touching, into an oiled steamer basket. Steam over boiling water, covered, 8 min. Remove ravioli with a spatula, one at a time — they will try to stick together. Make the sauce: melt butter in oil. Sauté garlic briefly. Add wine, boil gently 2-3 min. Remove from heat. Stir in parsley & lemon juice. Pour over ravioli. Top with black pepper & toasted pine nuts. ♥

"Manners must adorn knowledge, and smooth its way through the world."
Philip Dormer Stanhope,
♥ Earl of Chesterfield

SPINACH DIP

Makes 2+ cups

I have stuffed this mixture into hollowed-out cherry tomatoes & into sugar snap peas. It's perfect as a dip for cut-up fresh vegetables & with all kinds of crackers. ♥

1 10 oz. pkg. chopped spinach,
   thawed & drained
1½ c. sour cream
½ c. mayonnaise
½ c. minced red onion
2 cloves minced garlic
1 Tbsp. fresh lemon juice
½ tsp. hot pepper sauce
¼ tsp. nutmeg

Combine all ingredients; mix well. Cover & chill. ♥

"There is nothing wrong with the world that a sensible woman could not settle in an afternoon."
♥ Jean Giraudoux

FORTUNE COOKIES

350° Makes 24

Easy to make and taste better than store-bought (which STILL ain't _that_ great), but the best part is that YOU get to do the fortunes. They can be serious or funny (we have laughed to tears); quote books are a great source for ideas. ♥

3 egg whites	½ c. cake flour
½ c. white sugar	½ tsp. vanilla
¼ c. brown sugar	

Type 24 fortunes on thin strips of paper. Preheat oven to 350°. Put all ingredients in food processor & blend 10~15 seconds. Cover cookie sheets with parchment paper, then grease the paper. Do only four at a time, dropping by measured tablespoonfuls on cookie sheet. Bake 10 min. Immediately remove with spatula. The rough side should be on the inside of the cookie. Put the fortune in the middle of the cookie, fold it in half ~ bring corners up. Let oven cool completely to 200°. Put all the finished cookies back on cookie sheet & bake till completely browned, about ½ hr. Put one in the toe of each Christmas stocking, serve them at birthdays, send them in the mail; feel free to predict the future. ♥

This person deserves more than fortune cookies for dessert — A surprise in the freezer!

POTATO SKINS
WITH DIP
450° Serves Six

Who doesn't like potato skins? This is a very special dip & also tastes great with cold Roasted Green Beans (p.72). ♥

12 baking potatoes
5 green onions, chopped
1 clove garlic
½ c. parsley, chopped

3/4 c. mayonnaise
½ c. sour cream
1½ tsp. Worcestershire
3 drops Tabasco

Preheat oven to 450°. With a sharp knife, peel the potatoes lengthwise, taking a bit of potato with the skin, into 1" strips. (Save potatoes for salad or whatever.) Put the strips, skin side up, on a buttered cookie sheet. Bake 20 min. till golden; remove from oven, salt lightly & cool. Put all remaining ingredients into food processor or blender & mix till smooth. Cover & chill. Serve with potato skins at room temperature. ♥

" I never see any home cooking. All I get is fancy stuff."
Duke of Edinburgh

SALSA
Makes 2+ cups

Fresh homemade salsa is a far cry from most of the canned or bottled versions I've tasted. Serve it, along with a bowl of sour cream, as a dip for tortilla chips, as a topping for tacos, or with Quesadillas (p.116). ♥

3 lg. vine~ripened summer tomatoes,
   squeezed and finely chopped
3/4 c. green onions, chopped
3 Tbsp. green chilies, minced
   (use jalapeño if you want it hot)
1 Tbsp. cilantro, minced
½ tsp. celery seed
1 Tbsp. red wine vinegar
salt & freshly ground black pepper, to taste

Cut the tomatoes in half & squeeze the insides into a bowl. Finely chop them & add to the bowl with all other ingredients. Chill well before serving ♥.

"The right food always comes at the right time. Reliance on out-of-season foods makes the gastronomic year an endlessly boring repetition."
   ♥ Roy Andries De Groot

STUFFED EGGS

These are always a nice thing to serve along with all the "goo—goo" hors d'oeuvres — the men love them, they're substantial & there's never any left over.

hard-boiled eggs   minced celery
sweet pickle relish   dash Tabasco
celery seed   mayonnaise
freshly ground pepper   sweet pickle juice

Peel the hard-boiled eggs. (The fresher they are, the harder to peel.) Cut them in half lengthwise. Remove yolks to bowl. Put whites on serving dish. Mash yolks with potato masher & stir in all other ingredients (except pickle juice) to taste. If you need to thin it or if you like it sweeter, use the pickle juice (from the relish jar). Don't go overboard on the mayonnaise — it makes them boring. Taste as you go — pile yolk mixture back into whites. Refrigerate till time to serve. ♥

"Put all your eggs in one basket and
— WATCH THAT BASKET."
(The adorable) Mark Twain ♥

ESCARGOTS
450° Makes 1½ dozen

The perfect start for a French meal. Make sure you have some good French bread for mopping up the garlic butter. Shells & canned snails are available at gourmet food stores. For those that are alarmed at the idea of eating a snail, use a bite~sized piece of cooked sausage to fill the shell, but the truth is—the snails taste best! ♥

1½ dozen large snail shells
4½ oz. canned snails
½ c. butter, softened
¼ c. parsley, minced
4~5 cloves garlic, minced
2 shallots, minced
freshly ground pepper
pinch of nutmeg

Preheat oven to 450°. Rinse & drain shells; drain snails. Cream together all other ingredients. Put a snail in each shell, then fill to top with butter mixture. Heat them in the oven till bubbling hot. Serve with French bread ♥. Handy to have: metal snail dishes to balance the shells as they cook & some little 2~pronged forks to eat them with. ♥

SQUID

Serves Six

For those of us who still get flashbacks from the movie "20,000 Leagues Under the Sea," it's very hard to imagine EATING a squid. But they're light, chewy & <u>delicious</u>.

2 lbs. fresh squid, cleaned
flour for dredging
oil for frying
Garlic Tartar Sauce

Make the Tartar Sauce, cover & refrigerate. Rinse the squid (your fish-person will clean it). Slice the fish into 1/4" to 1/2" strips; pat dry with paper towels; dredge in flour. Fry quickly, a few at a time, in 1/2" very hot oil. Drain on paper towels. Serve warm with

Garlic Tartar Sauce

1½ c. mayonnaise
2 cloves garlic, minced
2 Tbsp. parsley, minced

1½ Tbsp. green onion, minced
2 Tbsp. capers
1 Tbsp. sweet pickle, minced
2½ Tbsp. cider vinegar

Mix all ingredients & refrigerate. ♥

BACON & CREAM-CHEESE TOMATOES

Makes about 50

about 3 pints cherry tomatoes, tops removed
2 8-oz. pkg. cream cheese, softened
12 slices bacon, crisply cooked & drained on paper towels
1/4 c. green onions, minced
1/4 c. parsley, minced
1/2 tsp. Worcestershire sauce

Hollow out cherry tomatoes with melon baller. Beat together cream cheese, crumbled bacon, onions, parsley & Worcestershire sauce. Stuff mixture into tomatoes. ♥

GARLIC & HERB POPCORN

Makes 1 big bowlful

1/3 c. popping corn
2 Tbsp. oil
1/3 c. butter
3 cloves garlic, minced
1 tsp. dry dillweed or thyme

Pop the popcorn in a big (3 qt.) pot in the 2 Tbsp. oil. Meanwhile, melt butter, add garlic & cook 1-2 min. Stir in dill; pour over popcorn & toss. ♥

"Beware of all enterprises that require new clothes." ♥ Henry David Thoreau

THE DO-IT-YOURSELF
ALL-APPETIZER
PARTY

It had been a good week at the old Branch homestead. Suddenly, unexpectedly, we had 6 hungry people in the house. We were sitting there eating this delicious variety of part leftovers, part spur-of-the-moment cooking, when it came to me that I ought to write it all down, mostly because it was being devoured with such obvious relish! It wasn't fancy or elegant but it was fun to watch how creative people could be with such an assortment ~ what they'd put with what ~ it was "oooo, try THIS!" It was spur of the moment ~ one of those lucky days when there's a ton of stuff in the refrigerator, but I'd even take the time to plan the exact same thing, that's why I wrote it down. ♥ So here's the "menu":

mustard, hot, & sweet
thin slices of rare steak
bermuda onion slices
pickles
smoked bluefish paté
French bread & crackers
apple slices
meat patés, country & smooth
celery stalks

cream cheese
smoked salmon
lemon & lime slices
roasted garlic ⎫ see p. 12
Montrachet ⎭
jar of sun-dried
    tomatoes
steamed shrimp & sauce
salt & pepper

This, plus some wine & beer & a quick Chocolate Fondue (p. 13), is a feast! Try it instead of a sit-down dinner ~ have all appetizers & eat in the kitchen. ♥

CHEESE

When you're too busy to cook, you can have very elegant hors d'oeuvres direct from your gourmet food store. They allow tasting; pick up your favorite cheese, a slice of beautiful paté, some gherkins & Greek olives — slice an apple & voilà : food! Here are some cheeses & ideas:

KASSERI: This cheese makes a delicious snack called "saganaki". Sauté slices in frying pan with a little butter. Serve sizzling hot with fresh lemon juice & pita or French bread. ♥

PARMIGIANO-REGGIANO: The very best Parmesan — from Italy. ♥

MONTRACHET: My favorite goat cheese (chèvre). Best when very fresh — it's moist & creamy. Sometimes in olive oil with thyme; delicious baked (see pg. 12) or broken over lettuce leaves, peppered & tossed with balsamic vinegar. ♥

EXPLORATEUR: Very rich — a triple cream cheese like St. Andre. Creamy & spreadable, it needs to be fresh. ♥

PORT SALUT: Semi-soft & smooth. The best has S.A.F.R. stamped on rind. Good with fruit — mild. ♥

FETA: There are lots of different ones — the creamier, milder ones come from Germany or Bulgaria. Good in salads. ♥

STILTON: This is an English cheese, a combination of cheddar & blue, so it has a little tang. ♥

MASCARPONE: From Italy, fresh, delicate, buttery. Good with fruit — pears & strawberries, ♥ especially.

SPRING

"Not a creature was stirring, not even a mouse" certainly fits for the quiet winter but in spring the creatures start stirring like mad. In April I start going out daily to see what's new. I lift some of the winter mulch to see the green shoots of the new plants ~ the mint is more than a survivor ~ I think it might be a predator! I even find it growing under the remains of the last snow. Spring is heard as much as seen ~ the birds & creatures are all so busy starting their families. It's time to air the quilts, think about the gardens, take off the storm windows, go for long walks & buy a new hat. It passes so quickly & in no time at all it's time to mow the first grass ~ what a wonderful smell that is. I think the island must look like a carpet of yellow from the air when the daffodils are in bloom. Spring is magic ~ sweet to the senses & easy to celebrate.

"May Day" is a charming custom that seems to have slipped in popularity, but when I was a child we used to make baskets out of woven strips of construction paper, tied with ribbons & filled with sugar cookies & with all the flowers we could find, both wild & not so wild (ahem!). Sometimes we'd make cornucopias out of old flowered wallpaper. On May 1st we'd place them on the front porches of favorite friends, ring the doorbell & run like crazy to hide & watch the surprise. I'm not sure who felt best, our friends ~ or us!

MORE  SPRING

❀ Use pink & yellow & green satin ribbons to tie around napkins, champagne glasses, invitations ~ makes a pretty table for Easter dinner. Paint names on colored eggs to use for placecards.

❀ Pack a picnic & take your family on a trip to the country. Visit a farm to see all the newborn baby animals.

❀ Air your blankets & quilts on a line in the yard, beat your rugs ~ take down heavy curtains & replace with something light & fluttery.

❀ Make a new bed in spring. Start with a thick mattress pad & some soft feather pillows ~ use fresh flowered sheets, a cotton comforter, a lace bed skirt. Open a nearby window to let in the sounds & smells of spring.

❀ Wild violets are one of the first spring flowers ~ they grow profusely & make the prettiest of small bouquets. For Mother's Day gather a corsage of violets, tie with a narrow satin ribbon, serve with hat pin to your mom.

❀ Plant radishes & let your children help. They are so easy & so quick that they are almost instant gratification & a good way to start young gardeners. Serve them sliced on buttered French bread, well salted & peppered.

❀ Make "sun tea" ~ put 5 tea bags in a half-gallon glass jar, fill with cold water & set it outside in the sun to steep. Serve it iced with lemon, sugar, & mint sprigs.

❀ Fly an American flag on Flag Day & Memorial Day. Get a tiny one for your car antenna for the trip to the Memorial Day picnic. ♥ It's spring, so sing it!

A Gift of Garlic

A wonderful, inexpensive gift for your friends — especially if you grow your own garlic. ♥ Just peel the cloves, put them in a jar, pour olive oil over just to cover, & seal jar. They keep for weeks in the refrigerator & it's so nice to have a supply of ready-to-use garlic & the added bonus of the garlic-flavored olive oil ♥.

SALADS

ICED SCALLOP SALAD

Serves Four

An elegant first course — for a light summer dinner include Lemon Noodles (p. 98), Roasted Green Beans (p. 72), & sautéed cherry tomatoes. ♥

1 lb. scallops
juice of 1 juicy lime
¼ c. watercress leaves
½ c. mayonnaise
2 Tbsp. green onion

2 Tbsp. parsley
1 tsp. fresh dill
2 tsp. lime juice
mixed salad greens

If you can't find the tiny Bay scallops, use the larger Sea scallops & cut them into bite~sized pieces. Rinse & drain them. Steam them in water just until done (don't overcook!). Drain, squeeze over lime juice, cover & chill. Put remaining ingredients (except greens) into food processor & process till smooth. Refrigerate. To serve: arrange greens on salad plates, divide scallops among them & top with a dollop of the lovely green sauce. ♥

Joey

COLE•SLAW

Serves Six

Bright, fresh & crisp. Serve a big bowl of this colorful salad for a picnic or barbecue. ♥

2 c. red cabbage, thinly shredded
2 c. green cabbage, thinly shredded
1 c. grated carrots
1 Tbsp. grated onion
¼ c. cider vinegar
¼ c. salad oil
1 Tbsp. brown sugar
¼ tsp. salt
freshly ground black pepper

Combine shredded cabbages, carrots, & onion in a large bowl. Whisk together vinegar, oil, brown sugar, salt, & pepper. Pour over salad & toss. Serve chilled. ♥

"Ten years ago the deficit on my farm was about a hundred dollars; but by well-designed capital expenditure, by drainage and by greater attention to details, I have got it into the thousands."
Stephen Leacock

FRESH FLOWER SALAD
With Vinaigrette

All of these flowers are easy to grow & they make a really pretty summer salad. Start a small salad garden of your own — grow leaf lettuce, garlic, chives, herbs, & flowers. That way you'll have everything perfectly fresh and unsprayed. The fresh flowers are becoming available in supermarkets & health food stores. ♥

violets & pansies in all colors
Johnny~jump~ups
nasturtiums, all colors
roses, wild or cultivated, petals only
forget~me~nots
parsley heads
curly~leafed endive
red lettuce (Salad Bowl)

Pick the flowers early in the day & refrigerate. They bruise easily so handle carefully. Put the lettuce in a salad bowl, add the parsley (stemmed & in chunks, not chopped). Dress & toss with Vinaigrette; strew flowers over & serve. ♥

Vinaigrette

minced garlic, mustard, pepper
1 part balsamic vinegar
3 parts olive oil
light cream

Mix the garlic, etc., with the vinegar. Beat in oil slowly. Add a little cream, mix well. ♥

FARMER
SALAD

Serves Four

1 c. sour cream or yogurt
1 c. cottage cheese
4 green onions, minced
10 radishes, sliced
1 cucumber, chopped
½ tsp. dill
½ tsp. celery seed
freshly ground pepper

Mix all ingredients. Chill. Serve on a bed of fresh greens. ♥

CRANBERRY SAUCE

Makes 3 Cups

A Thanksgiving tradition 🦃. I always receive compliments for this recipe. ♥ For a pretty, seasonal decoration, buy an extra pound of fresh cranberries; put them in an old wooden bowl or basket to set out for holiday color 🌲.

1 lb. fresh cranberries	3/4 c. sugar
1 apple, peeled, cored & chopped	½ c. water
2 lg. oranges, peeled & chopped	juice of 1 juicy lemon

Combine all ingredients in a heavy saucepan. Cover & cook over very low heat, stirring occasionally, for 3 or 4 hours. Serve hot or cold. Also good on sandwiches with turkey and stuffing. ♥

"I love everything that's old: old friends, old times, old manners, old books, old wines."
♥ Oliver Goldsmith

BEET SALAD

Serves Six

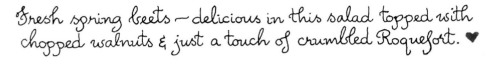

Fresh spring beets — delicious in this salad topped with chopped walnuts & just a touch of crumbled Roquefort. ♥

5 medium beets	½ c. sour cream
4 Tbsp. red wine vinegar	½ c. chopped walnuts
2 Tbsp. salad oil	Roquefort cheese, to taste
1 small red onion, sliced	Freshly ground pepper

Wash & trim beets. Cook in boiling water till tender. Drain & cool; peel them, cut into julienne strips. Put into bowl with thinly sliced onion & toss with vinegar & oil. Add the sour cream & mix gently. Sprinkle on walnuts, crumble on cheese & grind pepper over. Serve on a bed of torn salad greens if you like. ♥

SUMMER SALAD WITH ROSEMARY

Serves Four

Rosemary grows like a fiend, makes a wonderful ground cover, deters garden pests, & tastes like heaven in this delicious salad. ♥ Your local gourmet food store should be able to supply anything your regular market doesn't carry. ♥

½ lb. orzo pasta

1½ c. pine nuts, toasted

1 c. Montrachet or feta cheese

1 or 2 cloves garlic, minced

¼ c. fresh rosemary

¼ c. olive oil

juice from 1 lemon

1 c. Niçoise olives

Orzo is a tiny rice-like pasta, available in super-markets. Cook the orzo in boiling water, careful not to overcook; drain, rinse in cold water. Lightly brown pine nuts in butter; set aside to cool. Crumble (in big bits) the cheese over the pasta. Mince the garlic & rosemary & lightly toss all ingredients together except the olives. Refrigerate till ready to serve; then either put a few olives on each serving plate, or surround the salad bowl with them.

"There's rosemary, that's for remembrance; pray, love, remember..." ♥ Wm. Shakespeare

FRESH APPLESAUCE

Serves Four

Because it's not cooked, this applesauce has a wonderful fresh flavor—great for your kids. The frozen banana makes it icy cold, & you can blend it to the consistency you like, chunky or smooth. ♥

1 frozen banana
3 lg. green apples
¼ tsp. each cinnamon & nutmeg
½ c. apple juice

Peel, slice, wrap & freeze the banana. Peel the apples, set one aside, core & chop the other two. Put the frozen banana, the two chopped apples, cinnamon, nutmeg & juice into blender or food processor — blend till smooth. Remove to bowl & grate in the other apple. Stir & serve. ♥

"I have always maintained that there is nothing wrong with nursery food now that we are grown up and can have a glass of wine with it."
♥ Elizabeth Ray

PINE NUT SALAD

Serves Six

When it's your turn to bring the salad, bring this one! Served cold, it's fresh, flavorful & fun. *Yes*

2 c. pine nuts
2 Tbsp. butter
½ lb. alphabet pasta
1 c. black olives, sliced
½ c. parsley, minced
½ c. green onion, minced

⅓ c. green bell pepper
⅓ c. red bell pepper
¼ c. fresh lemon juice
¼ c. olive oil
Freshly ground pepper
Parmesan cheese, to taste

In a large skillet, lightly toast the pine nuts in the butter; drain on paper towels & cool. Cook the alphabet pasta in boiling water; drain & rinse in cold water. (Be extra careful not to overcook the pasta.) Very gently, mix together all ingredients; cover & chill. *Brrr*

"Little Willie from his mirror
Licked the mercury right off,
Thinking in his childish error,
It would cure the whooping cough.
At the funeral his mother
Smartly said to Mrs. Brown:
"Twas a chilly day for Willie
When the mercury went down.""
♥ Anonymous

RASPBERRIES & WATERCRESS

Serves Four

Beautiful in summer. ♥

1¼ c. fresh raspberries
¼ c. walnut or olive oil
grated rind of 1 orange
¼ c. fresh orange juice
3 tbsp. raspberry vinegar
1 tsp. honey
freshly ground pepper
1 c. walnuts, coarsely chopped & toasted
4 c. fresh watercress, tough stems removed
thinly sliced red onion

Force ¼ c. raspberries through a sieve & into shaker jar; add next six ingredients & shake well. Spread walnuts on cookie sheet & bake in 350° oven 5 min. until toasted. Toss together remaining raspberries, watercress, walnuts & red onion. Dress & serve. ♥

"Thou shalt sit on a cushion and sew a fine seam
and feed upon strawberries, sugar and cream." ♥
Anonymous

BUTTER LETTUCE SALAD
Serves Four

Soft lettuce, sun-dried tomatoes & fresh mushrooms in a hot dressing—a great beginning to any special meal—delicious with Sole Meunière (p.113).

½ c. sun-dried tomatoes in oil
olive oil, if needed
4 c. torn butter lettuce leaves
1 c. sliced mushrooms
¼ c. red wine vinegar
freshly ground pepper

Drain tomatoes; reserve oil & add enough olive oil (if necessary) to equal ½ cup. Sliver tomatoes & mix with lettuce. In a skillet, combine mushrooms with the oil; stir over high heat till hot; add vinegar, & pepper to taste. Pour over salad & toss lightly. Serve. ♡

♥ ♥ ♥ ♥ ♥

"I have been here before,
But when or how I cannot tell;
I know the grass beyond the door,
The sweet keen smell,
The sighing sound, the lights around the shore."
♡ Dante Gabriel Rossetti

GREEK POTATO SALAD

Serves Eight

I love any kind of potato salad but this one is especially good with the tart bits of Greek olives. ♥

2 lb. med. red potatoes
2/3 c. olive oil
1/3 c. red wine vinegar
1/2 tsp. oregano
1/2 tsp. rosemary, crumbled
1/2 lb. feta cheese, crumbled
1 sweet red pepper, seeded & chopped
1/2 c. green onion, chopped
1/2 c. Kalamata olives, pitted & chopped
salt & freshly ground pepper, to taste

Cook the potatoes in boiling water, jackets on, till tender. Drain thoroughly & put into lg. salad bowl. Coarsely cut them into bite-sized pieces. Mix together oil, vinegar, oregano, & rosemary; pour over potatoes. Add remaining ingredients; toss gently. Let stand 1/2 hr. so flavors marry. Serve at room temperature. ♥

"In all things of nature there is something of the marvelous." ♥
Aristotle

CHÈVRE SALAD

My favorite summer salad. The vinegar mixes with the cheese & makes a delicious fresh dressing; no oil! We take it to the beach in a covered bowl with 2 forks.

Toss together to taste:
soft lettuce, butter or Bibb
Montrachet cheese, crumbled
freshly ground pepper
Balsamic vinegar
cooked chicken, opt.

48

VELVET CHICKEN SALAD

Serves Four to Six

2 whole boned & skinned
  chicken breasts
4 Tbsp. cornstarch
2 egg whites
½ tsp. salt
2 tsp. light soy sauce
ice water
½ lb. snow peas
1 Tbsp. fresh ginger, minced

3 cloves garlic, minced
¼ c. toasted sesame seeds
¼ c. fresh lemon juice
¼ c. salad oil
1 Tbsp. light soy sauce
1 8½-oz. can pineapple
  chunks, drained
1 8 oz. can sliced water
  chestnuts, drained

Cut chicken in bite-sized pieces. In a med. bowl mix together cornstarch & egg whites; stir in chicken. In a saucepan, bring 3 qts. water, salt & soy sauce to a boil. Fill a large bowl with ice & water & set aside. Set a colander in the sink. Add chicken to boiling water — as soon as it comes back to the boil, remove from heat & let stand 1 minute. Drain in colander & immediately plunge chicken into ice water. Let it sit for 2 minutes; drain & put into salad bowl. Blanch snow peas in boiling water 1 min.; drain, rinse in cold water & add to salad bowl along with all other ingredients.

"The carp was dead, killed, assassinated, murdered in the first, second and third degree. Limp, I fell into a chair, with my hands still unwashed reached for a cigarette, lighted it, and waited for the police to come take me into custody." ♥ Alice B. Toklas

49

ORANGE & ONION

Ice-cold oranges, crisp red onion — make the perfect salad for Christmas dinner.

Per Person:
> 1 navel orange, peeled & sliced
> 1 slice red onion, in rings
> ½ Tbsp. olive oil
> a squeeze of fresh lime juice
> a grating of fresh black pepper

When you peel the oranges they should be cold & you should use a knife — make sure you remove all the white stuff from the outside of the orange. Arrange orange slices & onion rings on salad plates. Sprinkle olive oil & lime juice over them; grind on pepper. Serve chilled. ♥

"Most all the time, the whole year
round, there ain't no flies on me,
But jest 'fore Christmas
I'm as good as I kin be!"
                    ♥ Eugene Field

TWO GREAT SALAD DRESSINGS

Cream 'n' Bacon

Makes 1 cup

6 slices bacon
1 Tbsp. olive oil
⅓ c. shallots, minced
⅓ c. red wine vinegar
¾ c. heavy cream
freshly ground pepper

Fry the bacon crisp, remove and set aside. Pour out all but 1 Tbsp. bacon grease, add 1 Tbsp. olive oil & sauté shallots slowly till soft & golden. Scrape up any bits of bacon stuck to pan. Stir in vinegar, then cream. Mix well, heat through but don't boil. Crumble bacon over crisp cold greens & pour hot dressing over. Serve. Can be reheated.

Spicy Herb

Makes 1¼ cups

½ c. mayonnaise
½ c. sour cream
2 tsp. anchovy paste
2 Tbsp. tarragon vinegar

1 green onion
1 clove garlic
¾ c. parsley
1 Tbsp. fresh basil

Put all ingredients into blender or food processor & blend till smooth. Cover & chill

SUMMERTIME

In the summer the fireflies come out — they blink like a million tiny lights in the woods. I feel like they must be some sort of legacy from Walt Disney, master of the tiny light. Summer magic is everywhere on Martha's Vineyard. Sometimes it is so beautiful that as I walk or drive around it seems as if there are fairies running ahead to set up scenes just for my pleasure. ♥ Gardens go wild: the corn begins to ripen, the tomatoes turn red & sweet, the perennial garden is thick with summer bloom (the weeds go berserk, the lawn grows WAY too fast). ♥ There are picnics, outdoor concerts, & cookouts; beach trips, country fairs & jam making & there seems to be a rush for enjoyment — it all ends so soon. Summer dreams, summer schemes:

Take a day a month to visit local art galleries — there are special openings in the summer; they usually have wine & appetizers & some beautiful art. ♥

Early on summer mornings go to yard sales. Collect old creamers & sugar bowls for your flowers & plants. ♥

Wonderful: screened porches, unscreened porches, glassed porches & unglassed — with old wicker chairs, pots of geraniums — all bring romance to summer. ♥

...Summer Dreams & Schemes:

For the table: take tiny seashells & fill them with wet sand; poke in the stems of little flowers — one for each place setting. ♥

Plan a hot summer midnight supper on the beach or near a lake — a real expedition. Bring candles, music, blankets, pillows, champagne & cold oysters; chocolate truffles, St. Andre cheese & cold lobster meat. Enjoy a summer moon. ♥

Take your family berry picking — take baskets & buckets & get those berries. Make jam & berry pies.

Set an old chair or wicker rocker out in the garden. ♥

On a hot, hot day when everyone is quick to argue or too lazy to move — go get some root beer & some ice cream — make big root beer floats with long spoons & straws. Wash the car; be liberal with the hose. ♥

Pick a flower here and there — put them between the pages of a big heavy book to dry. Use them in cards & letters come winter. ♥

Shine up your indoor plants — wash the leaves with water & then rub each one with a tiny bit of mayonnaise. It doesn't hurt them a bit. ♥

"Summer afternoon — summer afternoon; to me those have always been the two most beautiful words in the English language." ♥
Henry James

"Strephon kissed me in the spring,
Robin in the fall,
But Colin only looked at me
And never kissed at all.
Strephon's kiss was lost in jest,
Robin's lost in play,
But the kiss in Colin's eyes
Haunts me night and day."
♥ Sara Teasdale

"There is a garden in her face
Where roses and white lilies grow."
♥ Thomas Campion

VEGETABLES

" Earth is here so kind, that just tickle her with a hoe and she laughs with a harvest." ♥ Douglas Jerrold

GARLIC & POTATOES

350° Serves Two

Roasted, the garlic becomes mellow & sweet, the potatoes take on the flavors of garlic and thyme. For a picnic or barbecue they can be made in individual foil packages. ♥

♥ Double or triple this recipe to serve more:
6~7 small red potatoes, quartered
10 whole large cloves garlic, unpeeled
2 Tbsp. good olive oil
sprinkle of thyme, or fresh thyme branches
1 Tbsp. white wine
good grinding of fresh black pepper
sprinkle of salt

Preheat oven to 350°. Put all ingredients into baking dish; dribble over olive oil & wine. Cover tightly with foil & bake 1 hour. Serve. (The garlic will slip right out of the skin — don't eat the skin. ☺) ♥

"From the dog's point of view his master is an elongated and abnormally cunning dog."
♥ Mabel Robinson

"JACK BE LITTLE" TINY PUMPKINS

350°

We had a Halloween dinner last year & started with a tiny pumpkin on each plate — it was the perfect beginning! They would also look (and taste) great for Thanksgiving.

1 miniature pumpkin per person
1 Tbsp. butter (each)
1 tsp. brown sugar
sprinkle of cinnamon & nutmeg

Preheat oven to 350°. Cut off the very top of each pumpkin — about a quarter of the way down. Scoop out the seeds & strings. Put butter, brown sugar, cinnamon & nutmeg in each pumpkin — put the tops back on. Place them on a cookie sheet & bake 45~55 min., till fork-tender. Serve. ♥

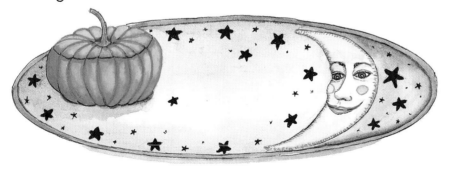

The official name for these pumpkins is "Jack Be Little Mini Pumpkins." ♥

APPLE & SWEET POTATO PURÉE

350° Serves Six

Serve this in late Fall with pork or chicken, at breakfast with sausage or bacon, or to your children for a healthy after~school tummy warmer. 🍎

2 medium sweet potatoes
6 Tbsp. unsalted butter
6 tart apples (Granny Smith), peeled, cored & sliced
½ tsp. cinnamon
1 Tbsp. fresh lemon juice
½ c. walnuts, chopped (opt.)

Bake the potatoes at 350° for 1 hour, till fork-tender. Cool to handle; cut in half, remove pulp, discard skins. In a large skillet, over med. heat, melt 1 Tbsp. of the butter. Add the apple slices; cover & cook for about 10~15 min., till soft & mushy. Put the apples, potato pulp, remaining butter, cinnamon & lemon juice in food processor & process till smooth. Serve hot with a sprinkle of walnuts, if desired. ♥ To reheat, put a little apple juice in a saucepan & heat slowly over low flame. ♥

"Part of the secret of success in life is to eat what you like and let the food fight it out inside." ♥ Mark Twain

SUMMER TOMATOES

Serves Four

My grandma used to make this for us with the wonderful fresh tomatoes from her garden. Don't bother with it unless you have the firm, vine-ripened tomatoes of summer. ♥

3 Tbsp. butter   2 Tbsp. basil, minced
1 med. onion, minced   2/3 c. heavy cream
4 good tomatoes, halved   fresh pepper

Sauté the onions slowly in the butter till soft & golden.   Put the tomatoes in the pan, cut side down, & sauté 5~7 min. Pierce skin with fork, turn them, sprinkle with basil. Cook 5 more min. Pour cream around tomatoes & boil. Add pepper to taste.   Spoon sauce onto plates, set tomato in center & serve. ♥

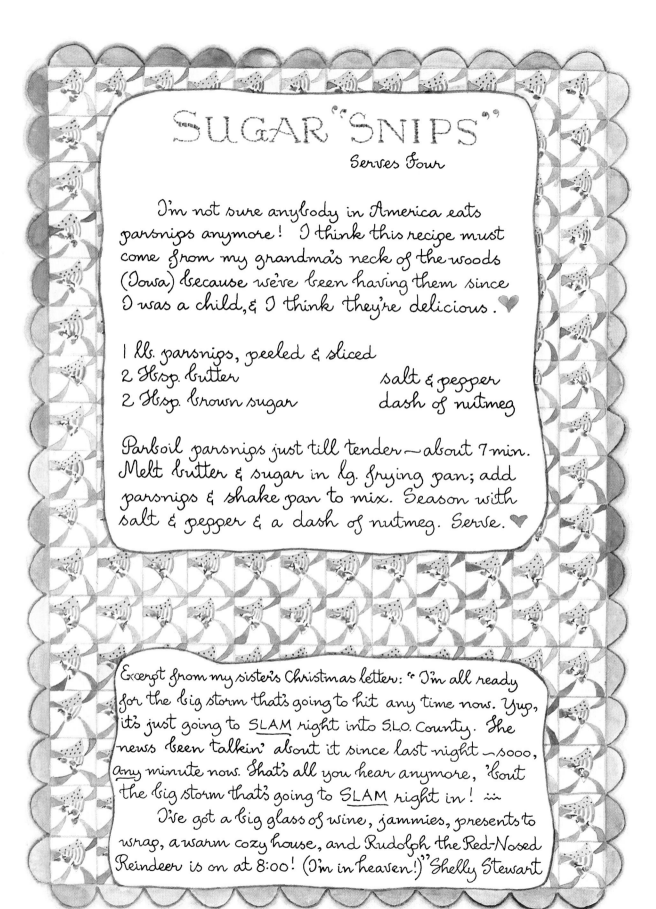

SUGAR "SNIPS"

Serves Four

I'm not sure anybody in America eats parsnips anymore! I think this recipe must come from my grandma's neck of the woods (Iowa) because we've been having them since I was a child, & I think they're delicious. ♥

1 lb. parsnips, peeled & sliced
2 Tbsp. butter
2 Tbsp. brown sugar

salt & pepper
dash of nutmeg

Parboil parsnips just till tender — about 7 min. Melt butter & sugar in lg. frying pan; add parsnips & shake pan to mix. Season with salt & pepper & a dash of nutmeg. Serve. ♥

Excerpt from my sister's Christmas letter: "I'm all ready for the big storm that's going to hit any time now. Yup, it's just going to SLAM right into S.L.O. County. The news been talkin' about it since last night — sooo, any minute now. That's all you hear anymore, 'bout the big storm that's going to SLAM right in! ∴
     I've got a big glass of wine, jammies, presents to wrap, a warm cozy house, and Rudolph the Red-Nosed Reindeer is on at 8:00! (I'm in heaven!)" Shelly Stewart

ASPARAGUS
in Mustard Cream Sauce
Serves Four

I finally planted asparagus. I was put off originally by the knowledge that I'd have to wait 2 years for my first harvest — but those 2 years, needless to say, passed anyway & my asparagus bed is now one of my garden "jewels." Every spring now, the tender spears come up to help us celebrate the season. Well worth the "wait."

¼ c. good dry white wine
½ c. heavy cream
1 tsp. Dijon mustard
3 Tbsp. butter
1½ lb. fresh asparagus

In a medium skillet, boil wine, heavy cream & mustard till reduced by half, stirring constantly. Stir in butter until melted; keep over low heat while you steam the asparagus till tender~crisp. Arrange asparagus & pour sauce over. Serve.

"The strongest of all warriors are these two — Time and Patience."
♥ Leo Tolstoi

SUCCOTASH

Serves Four to Six

This is an old favorite; nice texture between the corn & beans, sweetened with tomatoes & cream ♥. You could use fresh corn off the cob, fresh garden tomatoes & long cooked beans — it's wonderful that way. But, here I'm giving you the faster "winter version" — you can always have the ingredients on hand, & this delicious dish all year long ♥.

1 9~oz. pkg. frozen baby lima beans
1 10~oz. pkg. frozen corn
2 14~oz. cans whole tomatoes (2 c. fresh, peeled
    and chopped)
4 Tbsp. butter
⅓ c. heavy cream
salt & freshly ground pepper, to taste

Cook the lima beans in boiling water 10 min. Add corn & cook 3 min. longer, drain. Drain the tomatoes. Melt butter in large skillet; add corn, beans, & tomatoes — stir, breaking the tomatoes up with the spoon. Stir in cream & salt & pepper. Heat through and serve ♥

"Don't part with your illusions. When they are gone, you may still exist, but you have ceased to live." ♥ Mark Twain

SPINACH & HEARTS

350° Serves Six

The perfect vegetable for Valentine's !

2 red bell peppers
2 pkg. frozen chopped
    spinach, thawed
1 Tbsp. butter
⅓ c. shallots, minced
¾ c. Swiss cheese, grated
1 Tbsp. Romano cheese

½ c. fresh breadcrumbs
¼ tsp. nutmeg
4 beaten eggs
¼ c. milk
½ c. heavy cream
freshly ground pepper,
    to taste

Cut out 6 1-inch hearts from the peppers. Thaw, drain, & squeeze the spinach. Preheat oven to 350° & oil 6 custard cups. Put a heart into the bottom of each cup, skin down. Put butter & shallots into skillet~cook slowly till tender. Put into large bowl with cheeses, crumbs & nutmeg; add beaten eggs; mix well. Slightly warm the milk & cream & beat into egg mixture; stir in spinach, add pepper. Pour into cups. Put them into lg. pan; place pan in lower part of oven & add 1½ in. hot water to pan. Bake 40 min., till knife comes out clean. Cool, out of water, for a few minutes. Cut tightly around sides with sharp knife. Invert onto plates. ♥

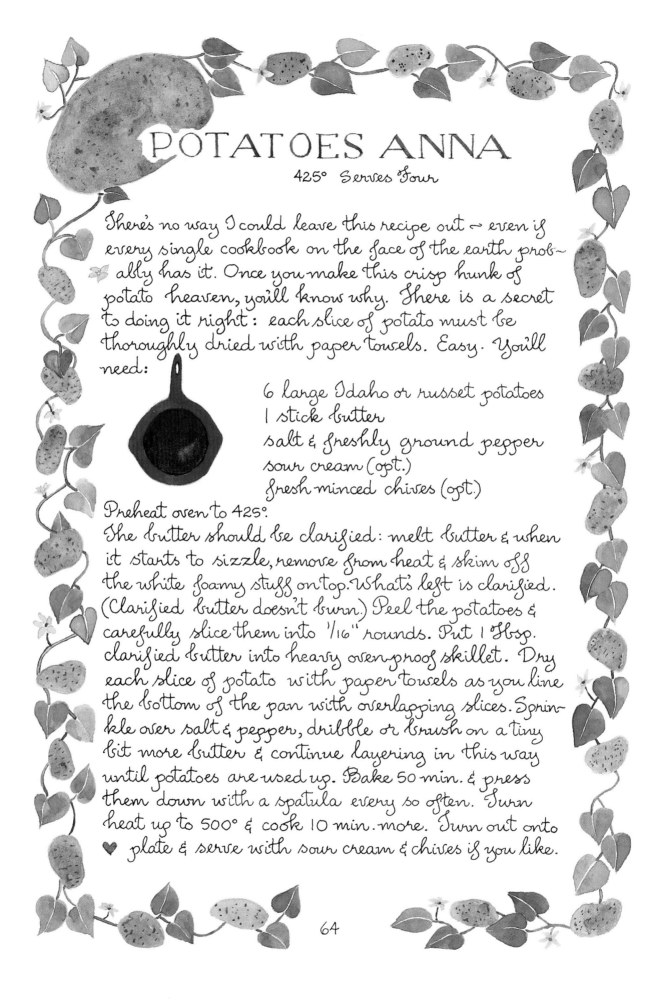

POTATOES ANNA

425° Serves Four

There's no way I could leave this recipe out ~ even if every single cookbook on the face of the earth prob-ably has it. Once you make this crisp hunk of potato heaven, you'll know why. There is a secret to doing it right: each slice of potato must be thoroughly dried with paper towels. Easy. You'll need:

6 large Idaho or russet potatoes
1 stick butter
salt & freshly ground pepper
sour cream (opt.)
fresh minced chives (opt.)

Preheat oven to 425°.
The butter should be clarified: melt butter & when it starts to sizzle, remove from heat & skim off the white foamy stuff on top. What's left is clarified. (Clarified butter doesn't burn.) Peel the potatoes & carefully slice them into 1/16" rounds. Put 1 Tbsp. clarified butter into heavy oven-proof skillet. Dry each slice of potato with paper towels as you line the bottom of the pan with overlapping slices. Sprin-kle over salt & pepper, dribble or brush on a tiny bit more butter & continue layering in this way until potatoes are used up. Bake 50 min. & press them down with a spatula every so often. Turn heat up to 500° & cook 10 min. more. Turn out onto plate & serve with sour cream & chives if you like.

MUSHROOM PANCAKES
Serves Four

Crisp little critters; delicious served with a little sour cream.

2 c. minced mushrooms
2 eggs, beaten
1 c. grated cheddar cheese
1/4 c. minced green onions
1/2 c. unbleached flour

1/2 tsp. baking powder
1/2 tsp. salt
1/4 tsp. thyme
1 Tbsp. oil
sour cream, garnish

Mince mushrooms (in food processor) & wring in towel to remove excess moisture. Beat eggs, add cheese, onions, & mushrooms. Combine dry ingredients & stir into mushroom mixture. Heat oil & drop mixture into skillet by tablespoonfuls. Brown on both sides. Serve with sour cream. ♥

SUMMER CORN

For a very large group at a barbecue, it's nice to serve the corn on the cob this way ~ no fights at the butter dish! ♥

Husk the corn, butter well with softened butter; salt & pepper. Wrap each piece in aluminum foil. Bake in 400° oven for 10~15 min. till heated through. ♥

CABBAGE WITH CARAWAY & BACON

Serves Four

Have this with a pork roast & some ice-cold Cranberry Sauce (pg. 40) for a delicious dinner in winter. ♥

    4 slices bacon
    ½ Tbsp. vegetable oil
    4 c. shredded cabbage
    1 Tbsp. caraway seeds
    2 Tbsp. cider vinegar
    salt & freshly ground pepper, to taste

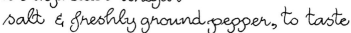

Cook bacon till crisp; drain on paper towels. In a large skillet with a cover, heat oil. Add cabbage, toss to coat with oil. Cover, reduce heat, cook till tender, stirring occasionally (10~15 min.). Sprinkle over caraway seeds, vinegar, & salt & pepper. Toss. Crumble bacon over & serve. ♥

STEAMED SPINACH

Serves Two

It's easy, very healthy, and my favorite. ♥

Wash & stem one large bunch spinach. Put it in a large saucepan with a little water & steam till wilted. Drain. Serve with a splash of cider or balsamic vinegar. Add toasted sesame seeds, if desired.

PEAS & CARROTS COPENHAGEN

Serves Four

I ate this every single day I was in Copenhagen, dissected it & brought it home  Now I serve it at Easter Dinner & every other time I want something special 🖤

2 carrots
1 10-oz. pkg. frozen baby peas
½ c. sour cream
1 Tbsp. fresh lemon juice
2 tsp. fresh chives, chopped
1 Tbsp. fresh dill, minced
freshly ground pepper to taste

Cut the carrots into sticks — steam till tender & refresh in cold water. Cook & drain peas. Cube carrots into pea-sized pieces. Mix together peas, carrots & all other ingredients. Chill. ❤️

"Mid pleasures and palaces
though we may roam,
Be it ever so humble, there's
no place like Home."
❤️ J. Howard Payne

POTATO HEAVEN

Serves One

Do you feel blue? Do you need a hug, a cuddle, a love? Then this is for you, from me, with T.L.C. It's perfect on rainy days & almost cures heartache.

Take about 1½ c. leftover mashed potatoes & form them in a nice firm little pancake. Dip it in flour. Melt butter in a small skillet; put the potato in. Cover & cook slowly till browned; turn, add more butter if necessary, continue cooking till other side is done. (Make hot chocolate while it cooks.) Put the potato on a plate, salt it, pepper it, add another chunk of butter — gather your flannel p.j's around you — head for bed.

"My soul is crushed, my spirit sore;
I do not like me anymore.
I cavil, quarrel, grumble, grouse.
I ponder on the narrow house.
I shudder at the thought of men. . .
I'm due to fall in love again."
                                        Dorothy Parker

FIDDLEHEAD
FERNS

I'm always excited to find something wonderful that I've never tasted before — last spring I found fiddlehead ferns. I'm not sure how available they are in the rest of the country, but I guarantee that very soon they'll be everywhere — they are so delicious. They're easy to grow, a perennial that comes up in my backyard every year with no coaxing. It is the very top of the fern, when it first comes up, all rolled up before it unfurls into fronds. You can steam them & serve with butter & salt & pepper, put them in salads, use them on a crudité plate, stir-fry them. They scream spring — if you find them on a menu or in a market, consider yourself blessed ♥.

"Throw a lucky man into the sea,
and he will come up with a fish
in his mouth."
♥ Arab Proverb

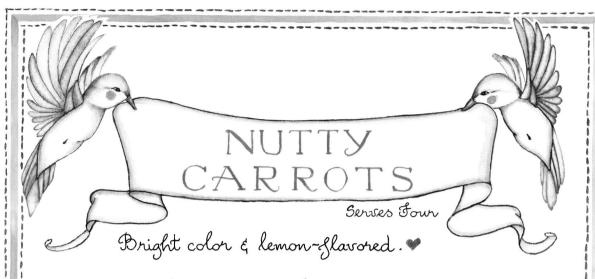

NUTTY CARROTS

Serves Four

Bright color & lemon-flavored. ♥

2/3 c. walnuts, coarsely chopped
4 fresh carrots
2 Tbsp. butter, melted
1/8 tsp. grated lemon peel
1 Tbsp. fresh lemon juice
1 tsp. honey
freshly ground pepper

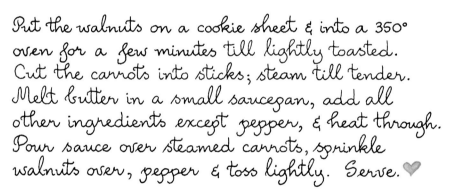

Put the walnuts on a cookie sheet & into a 350°
oven for a few minutes till lightly toasted.
Cut the carrots into sticks; steam till tender.
Melt butter in a small saucepan, add all
other ingredients except pepper, & heat through.
Pour sauce over steamed carrots, sprinkle
walnuts over, pepper & toss lightly. Serve. ♥

"The true way to soften
one's troubles is to solace
those of others." ♥
                  Mme. de Maintenon

CELERY

I love the flavor of cooked celery — this is an especially easy & delicious side dish.

½ c. slivered almonds
1 Tbsp. butter

3 Tbsp. butter
1 clove garlic, minced
4 c. celery, sliced in thin 1" strips
5 green onions, chopped

Sauté the almonds in 1 Tbsp. butter till light brown. Drain on paper towels & set aside. Melt 3 Tbsp. butter in large skillet. Over low heat, add garlic, celery, & onions; sauté gently, stirring often. Cook until celery is tender — crisp, top with almonds & serve.

If you like cream cheese with your celery & don't mind a few jillion extra calories, try this sauce: melt 6 Tbsp. cream cheese with 6 Tbsp. milk till hot & creamy. Pour over celery & top with toasted almonds.

"Heaven will be no heaven to me if I
do not meet my wife there."
Andrew Jackson

ROASTED GREEN BEANS

500° Serves Four

Try these roasted beans cold too — they make a great hors d'oeuvre when served with the Dip on p. 24 ♥

1 lb. fresh green beans
1½ Tbsp. olive oil
fresh lemon juice
freshly ground pepper

Preheat oven to 500°. Trim the beans, spread on a cookie sheet, drizzle with oil & bake for 6~8 min. till tender, turning them occasionally. Remove to serving dish, squeeze lemon juice over, pepper & serve. Good hot or cold. ♥

ZUCCHINI WITH APPLE

Serves Four +

A tasty side dish — we had it last night with the Pasta & Grilled Sausages (p. 106) & Fresh Applesauce (p. 43) and it was wonderful for a chilly autumn evening. ♥

½ c. walnut pieces
¼ c. butter
2 small zucchini, grated
1 green apple, peeled & grated
fresh lemon juice
salt & pepper, to taste

Sauté the walnuts in butter over low heat till brown. Take the nuts out of the pan & set aside. Put the grated zucchini in the pan & sauté for 1 minute only. Remove from heat, add walnuts, grated apple & a few drops of lemon juice — stir & taste. Sprinkle on salt & pepper & serve. ♥

"The reader who is illuminated is, in a real sense, the poem." ♥
H. M. Tomlinson

FALL

The first time I came to New England, it was Fall & I fell completely in love. ♥ There was a delicious nip in the air as we drove along country roads, the leaves whipping in the wind, through woodland valleys that smelled of the earth, near lakes, brooks & streams all reflecting the flaming colors of the changing season, past the festive roadside stands filled with apples, pumpkins, & cider. ♥ We stopped at wonderful tiny restaurants in old houses with slanted floors & ate delicious soups, hot puddings bathed in cream & bowls of fresh raspberries 🍇. We saw the geese flying in formation & smoke curling out of 200-year-old chimneys. New England holds the key to American history; it can also hold the key to your heart, especially in the fall. ♥

CELEBRATE AUTUMN: Put a pumpkin on your porch — use bowls of nuts & apples to decorate.
🎃 Get the last of those vine-ripened sweet summer tomatoes & make your own tomato sauce to freeze for winter. Visit an apple farm — make applesauce & can it for Christmas presents And don't forget the blueberries & raspberries to freeze for winter pies.
🎃 Have a morning tea party — light the fire — float small apples studded with cloves in hot cider. Serve home-made toast with honey butter & breakfast sausage cooked in maple syrup.

~Fall~

🎃 Plan ahead & think of some really special & fitting words to bless your Thanksgiving dinner & family.

🎃 Make soups — they bubble softly, warm your house with delicious aromas & comfort your tummy on a chilly night.

🎃 Start planning for next summer's family reunion. Make & send invitations so that all, near & far, will have time to plan to come.

🎃 Save all your wine corks. You can glue them onto a piece of plywood to make a wonderful corkboard for your kitchen.

🎃 Go to a football game — take a warm blanket & a thermos of hot chocolate to share. (Hot chocolate is delicious with peppermint schnapps in it.)

🎃 Make a picture wall of family & friends. Mount your photos on matte board with spray glue. People love looking at them.

🎃 Halloween: I have a black iron cat I like to put on the porch with the scary~faced carved pumpkins — or get a big cardboard skeleton for your door. Have a Halloween dinner — serve the "Jack Be Little" Tiny Pumpkins on p. 57, & Witches' Brew, p.136.

"An' all us other children,
    when the supper things is done,
We set around the kitchen fire
    an' has the mostest fun
A-list'nin' to the witch~tales
    'at Annie tells about,
An' the gobble~uns 'at gits you
Ef you Don't Watch Out!"
James Whitcomb Riley

GIFT IDEAS
for those who have "Everything"

Antique stores are wonderful places — when you see some small perfect little thing, buy it & tuck it away for just the right moment. ♥ More ideas:

Tickets to something special — a play, concert or ball game.

Trees: cherry, walnut, lemon, apple or pear. There are also some elegant little miniatures to grow inside.

Homemade tapes of their favorite music.

One especially gorgeous sterling silver serving piece wrapped in beautiful paper. (I love the tissue paper Victoria's Secret uses & save it for this.)

An old book — something of interest to the person — beautifully bound & papered.

Their favorite newspaper — issued on the day & year of their birth.

Save all your Sweetheart roses & dry them by hanging upside down. Give potpourri in a delicate glass bowl & include lots of the dried roses.

Enlarged photos of themselves or their loved ones (kids, boat, car?).

A beautiful old flowered teacup & saucer.

For Christmas this year I was given a darling bowl with crocus getting ready to bloom — it's now the middle of January & I check on it & admire it everyday. I just love it — a kind of continuing present. (Thanks, Peg ♥)

SOUPS

"To love what you do and feel that it matters —
how could anything be more fun?" ♥
Katharine Graham

SPLIT PEA SOUP

Serves Ten

A hearty soup to warm the tummy ♥.

2 large ham hocks
1 lb. split peas, rinsed
2 med. onions, chopped
3 stalks celery, chopped
3 carrots, chopped
1 clove garlic, minced

1 bay leaf
½ tsp. oregano
1 tsp. dry mustard
1 tsp. salt
8 c. cold water
5 strips bacon

Put everything but the bacon in a soup pot. Bring to a boil, reduce heat, cover & simmer for 2 hours, stirring occasionally. Remove ham hocks, take off meat & cut in pieces. Put the meat back in the soup. Fry up the bacon crisp & either put it in the soup or use it to garnish each serving. ♥ The soup can either be thinned with water or thickened by boiling away liquid with the lid off.

"There are fairies at the bottom of our garden!"
♥ Rose Fyleman

WATERCRESS & ORANGE SOUP

Serves Four

Serve this refreshing cold soup for the first course in a springtime dinner. The orange flavor is subtle & elegant. ♥

2 bunches watercress, chopped
2½ c. chicken broth
2 Tbsp. fresh chives, chopped
1 egg yolk
1 c. heavy cream
freshly ground pepper
1 c. fresh orange juice
2 Tbsp. Grand Marnier

Simmer watercress, chicken broth & chives together for ½ hour. Blend mixture in food processor till smooth. Reheat mixture (don't boil). Whisk egg yolk & cream together. Mix a little of the hot soup into the cream; pour the cream into the soup & stir until hot. Grind over pepper to taste. Refrigerate soup until well chilled. Just before serving stir in fresh orange juice & Grand Marnier. If you like, sprinkle on fresh chives, or use a thin slice of orange or a sprig of fresh watercress for garnish. ♥

"One day in the country / Is worth a month in town." ♥ Christina Rossetti

CHINOIS SOUP

The little ginger-filled crepes tied up with chives
look darling floating in this delicious light broth.
This looks complicated to make, but it's really not.
The filled crepes can be made ahead. ♥

Crepes

Makes 10 5" crepes

1 beaten egg
½ c. milk

scant ½ c. flour
1 Tbsp. melted butter

Add milk to beaten egg; gradually whisk in
flour, till smooth. Beat in butter. Lightly oil 7"
sauté pan, HEAT till moderately hot. Pour about 3 Tbsp.
batter into pan & quickly swirl to coat bottom.
Lightly brown, turn to cook other side. Finish all
& make

Filling

3/4 c. waterchestnuts
4 green onions, tops only
3 tsp. fresh ginger
10 long whole chives

Mince finely first 3
ingredients. Put 1 tsp. of
mixture in center of each
crepe. Tie into little bag
with whole chive.

Soup

5 c. homemade or canned chicken broth
1½ Tbsp. light soy sauce
2 tsp. sesame oil
Bring all ingredients to a boil.
Put 2 filled crepes into each
soup bowl — ladle hot soup
over & serve.

VEGETABLE & CHEESE SOUP

Serves Four

Everybody loves this soup. ♡ It's creamy with little bits of vegetables. I like to serve it with either cucumber sandwiches or buttered French bread & radishes. ♡

2 Tbsp. butter
1 leek, chopped
2 carrots, sliced
1 sm. onion, chopped
1 stalk celery, chopped
1 Tbsp. cornstarch
3 Tbsp. flour
2 c. milk

1 13¾-oz. can chicken broth
1 ⅓ c. grated cheddar cheese
½ tsp. salt
2 Tbsp. parsley, minced
2 Tbsp. chives, chopped
pinch of cayenne pepper
⅛ tsp. baking soda

Melt butter in large saucepan. Add leek, carrots, onion & celery; sauté slowly until soft. Stir in cornstarch & flour, blending well. In another pan heat milk & broth together; add to vegetables. Cook over medium heat until thickened. Purée mixture in food processor. Return mixture to saucepan; add cheese, salt, parsley, chives & cayenne. Stir till cheese is melted. Add baking soda to lighten. Serve hot. ♡

CHILLED CUCUMBER
& TOMATO SOUP

Serves Four

I liken this to gazpacho, but creamy. It's wonderful in the summer.

3 cucumbers, peeled & coarsely chopped
¼ c. parsley (no stems)
½ c. green onions, chopped
2 cloves garlic, minced
1 c. tomato juice (or V-8)
1 c. chicken broth
3 tbsp. cider vinegar
2 c. sour cream
salt & freshly ground pepper, to taste
sliced cherry tomatoes, for garnish

Put the cucumbers, parsley, green onions, garlic, tomato juice, chicken broth, & vinegar into food processor & blend well. Pour into large bowl; add sour cream & salt & pepper to taste & mix together. Serve, garnished with sliced cherry tomatoes. ♥

"A knight errant who turns mad for a reason deserves neither merit nor thanks. The thing is to do it without cause."

Miguel de Cervantes

GARLIC SOUP

Serves Four

Garlic's good for you! ♥

20 cloves garlic (yup! 20)
2 onions, sliced
1½ Tbsp. olive oil
3 c. tomatoes, peeled & chopped
2 c. tomato juice
2 c. beef broth
8 ½" slices French-bread baguette, toasted
4 oz. Swiss cheese, grated

Blanch garlic cloves in boiling water 30 seconds, rinse in cold water, drain, peel, slice thin. In a large saucepan, sauté the onions in oil till soft & golden, about 15 min. Add garlic, tomatoes, & tomato juice. Bring to boil; reduce heat, cover and simmer 30 min. Add the beef broth — bring to boil, ladle into ovenproof bowls. Top with toast, then cheese. Put into 450° oven till cheese is melted. Serve ♥

"My kitchen is a mystical place, a kind of temple for me. It is a place where the surfaces seem to have significance, where the sounds and odors carry meaning that transfers from the past and bridges to the future."
Pearl Bailey ♥

BORSCHT
Serves Six

Very easy, beautiful color & good for you. Serve it with pickled herring in sour cream, red onion slices & some good pumpernickel bread. A little Russian feast. ♥

2 c. beets, peeled & chopped
1 lg. onion, chopped
2 carrots, thinly sliced
2 celery ribs, thinly sliced
2 c. cabbage, shredded
2 lg. potatoes, diced
4 c. beef broth
4 c. water
2 c. tomato purée
2 cloves garlic, minced
1 bay leaf
salt & freshly ground pepper
sour cream for garnish, opt.

Combine all ingredients, except salt, pepper, & sour cream, in large soup pot. Bring to a boil & simmer about 1½ hours. Remove bay leaf, add salt & pepper to taste & serve with a spoonful of sour cream. ♥

"Soup is sensitive. You don't catch steak hanging around when you're poor and sick, do you?" ♥ Judith Martin

Turkey Soup

Waste not, want not. ♥ We had a 22 lb. bird this year, which gave me about 20 cups of stock — so I froze 10 for later & last night I made the first batch. ♥

The Stock: Pick all the meat off the carcass & reserve. Put the carcass in a big pot & add a couple of carrots, 1 onion, 2 stalks celery, a handful of parsley — all unpeeled, but washed & coarsely chopped. Add a few peppercorns, a bay leaf or two. Add water to cover, boil; then cover and simmer 6—10 hours. Strain, refrigerate overnight, uncovered. Remove fat from top of stock.

Soup

10 c. stock
1 med. onion, chopped
2 stalks celery, chopped
2 carrots, chopped
1 Tbsp. olive oil
1 Tbsp. butter
turkey meat, chopped

¼ c. parsley, chopped
1 tsp. basil
½ tsp. thyme
½ tsp. sage
4 oz. egg noodles
salt & pepper

Bring stock to boil, taste for strength — if weak, boil down. Sauté onion, celery & carrots in oil & butter. Add rest of ingredients to stock. When noodles are done, add vegetables & serve. ♥ This is great "diet food" after holiday debaucheries ♥.

"So once in every year we throng
   Upon a day apart,
To praise the Lord with feast and song
   In thankfulness of heart." ♥
Arthur Guiterman

HOT APPLE SOUP

You can even serve this soup for brunch — it's a Fall soup, when apples are a part of the celebration ♥.

4 green apples (Granny Smith)   ½ tsp. cinnamon
4 McIntosh apples   1 c. light cream
2½ c. water   unsweetened whipped
2 Tbsp. lemon juice   cream, for garnish
¼ tsp. nutmeg

Peel, core & quarter apples. Combine all ingredients except cream in saucepan & bring to boil. Simmer 15 min. till apples are soft. Purée; return to pan; add cream & heat through but don't boil. Garnish each serving with a dollop of unsweetened whipped cream & a sprinkle of cinnamon. ♥

"On a windy day let's go flying
There may be no trees to rest on
There may be no clouds to ride
But we'll have our wings and the
   wind will be with us
That's enough for me, that's enough
   for me."   Yoko Ono

MANY MUSHROOMS SOUP

Serves Four to Six

There are so many kinds of mushrooms available today, shapes, colors & textures. Take your pick for this beautiful soup. ♥

3 Tbsp. butter
3 Tbsp. oil
1 clove garlic, minced
1 onion, chopped
1 lb. mixed mushrooms
  (oyster, morels, porcini,
   enoki, brown or common — your choice)

3 c. chicken broth
1/4 c. white port
2 Tbsp. tomato paste
1/2 c. parsley, minced
pepper, to taste

Melt butter & oil in lg. saucepan. Sauté garlic & onion slowly over low heat, 10 min. Add sliced mushrooms, cover & cook over med. heat 5 min. Add broth, port & tomato paste. Simmer 10 min. Add parsley & freshly ground pepper. Serve. ♥

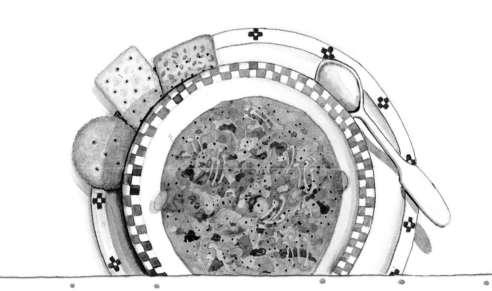

89

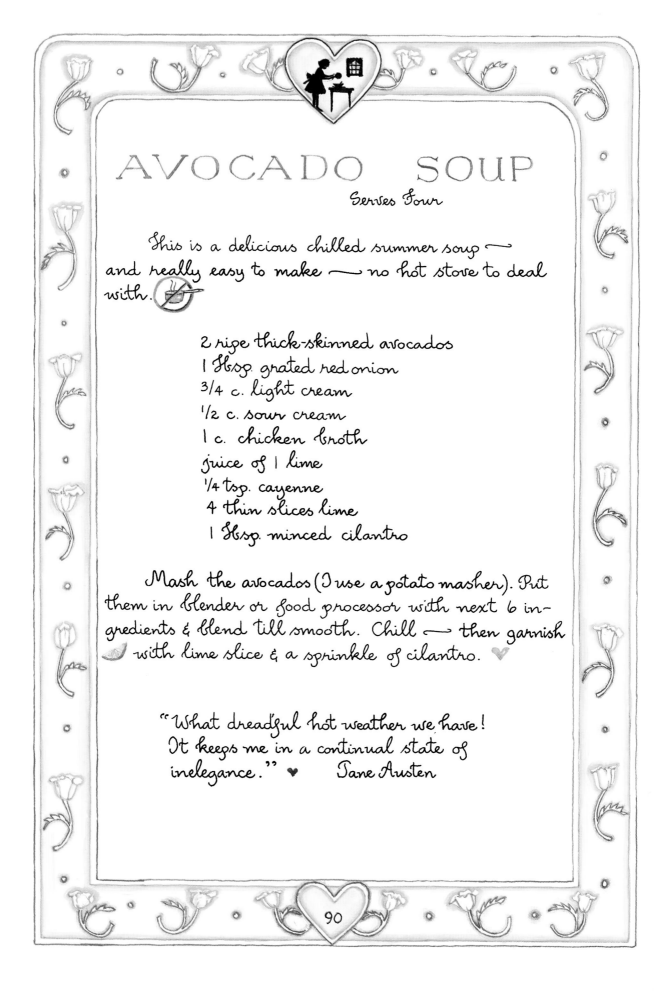

AVOCADO SOUP

Serves Four

This is a delicious chilled summer soup — and really easy to make — no hot stove to deal with.

2 ripe thick-skinned avocados
1 Tbsp. grated red onion
3/4 c. light cream
1/2 c. sour cream
1 c. chicken broth
juice of 1 lime
1/4 tsp. cayenne
4 thin slices lime
1 Tbsp. minced cilantro

Mash the avocados (I use a potato masher). Put them in blender or food processor with next 6 ingredients & blend till smooth. Chill — then garnish with lime slice & a sprinkle of cilantro.

"What dreadful hot weather we have! It keeps me in a continual state of inelegance." ❤ Jane Austen

LOBSTER BISQUE

Serves Six

A delicate peach-colored soup, not as heavy as some I've tasted but still extravagant & wonderful ♥.

3 Tbsp. butter
½ c. shallots, minced
4 c. chicken broth
1 bay leaf
¼ tsp. thyme
3 Tbsp. flour

2 Tbsp. tomato paste
¾ c. dry white wine
1 lb. cooked lobster
   meat
1½ c. half & half
1 Tbsp. cognac

Melt butter in lg. saucepan & sauté shallots till tender, over low heat. Meanwhile, bring chicken broth, bay leaf, & thyme to a boil in another pan. Whisk flour into shallot mixture, cook, stirring, 1-2 min. Stir in tomato paste; slowly whisk in boiling broth. Gradually add wine; simmer 10 min., stirring occasionally. Chop lobster meat, reserving a few nice pieces for garnish. Put the chopped meat & soup into food processor & blend. Return to pot, stir in half & half, then cognac. Heat through, garnish with lobster & serve. ♥

"The advantage of doing one's praising for oneself
   is that one can lay it on so thick and exactly
   in the right places."
                              ♥ Samuel Butler

WINTER

Winter in New England is a special treat for me ~ it's when the island is quietest ~ time seems to stand still except for when the holidays roll around & then it goes too quickly. I especially like it because it feels like a time to reflect & work ~ to sit by a warm fire, watch a quiet snowfall with birds & squirrels busy at the feeders. Here are some ideas to help you celebrate winter:

Save all of your children's mittens ~ even if you don't have both of them ~ from when they are babies. By the time they are 6 or 7 you'll have a lovely collection of winter memories to frame & hang on your wall.

Once a month stand in the exact same position outside your home & take a picture of your house & yard. Frame all the pictures together for a wonderful seasonal collage. ★

If you live in snow country, make your Christmas cards by using fresh cranberries & holly to write your message in the snow; photograph it & make as many copies as you'll need. Send them out as postcards. ♥

A tradition I've always loved: Have family and friends join hands at midnight on New Year's Eve & say a special prayer for the coming year. "Auld Lang Syne" by Guy Lombardo is a special touch to help welcome the new year. 🔔

For Dad on Valentine's: a personalized card. Put lipstick on you & your little ones ~ everybody kisses the card. 💋

92

Keep a fire burning ~ it's such a nice welcome for holiday guests or anytime. ♥

Put out baskets & bowls of fresh cranberries, bright red apples, lemons studded with cloves, nuts in their shells, potpourri, pomegranates, or fresh holly.

Use brightly colored quilts for tablecloths ~ have lots of candles burning.

For Christmas Eve Dinner hang a stocking on the back of each guest's chair ~ fill with funny & special gifts pertaining to the interests of the guest. Open them, with coffee & dessert, one at a time.

Simmer herbs & spices for good holiday smells ~ and play "The Nutcracker" at Christmas Brunch. ♪

For the Christmas table tie together tiny bunches of mistletoe with narrow satin ribbons & tuck in a placecard for each guest.

Make sure all your friends get home safely from holiday parties. ♥

The best gifts are handmade ~ gifts of food, knitted, embroidered or quilted things; wooden things & painted & drawn things ~ whatever you're good at. Encourage your children to be creative too.

Sleigh rides, Christmas caroling, tree cutting parties with popcorn & cranberry stringing to follow, old toys for decoration ~ I could go on forever ♥ Merry Xmas!

"What is patriotism good things we but the love of the ate in our childhood."
♥ Lin Yutang

KID STUFF

Memories . . . the food of our childhood; food that meant love ♥

On Valentine's Day we felt especially loved when we woke to a breakfast of hot cereal, tinted pink with food coloring & sprinkled with those little red Cinnamon Hearts.♥

Jell-O Oranges: Use a 6 oz. pkg. of Jell-O —what kind? RED!! Make according to pkg. instructions except use only 1½ c. boiling water (instead of 2). Hollow out halved oranges & fill with Jell-O. This makes 10 halves. Chill well & serve with a dot of whipped cream.

Purple Cow: a good summer drink — so nice & purple! Put a scoop of vanilla ice cream in a tall glass; fill up halfway with grape juice & top with fizzy water.

Rice Krispie Treats: kids know this is kids' food —but I still like 'em too. Melt ¼ c. butter in large saucepan —add 40 lg. marshmallows & stir till melted. Stir in 5 c. Rice Krispies. Press into 9"x 13" pan & chill.

Adventure Food: when your kids go off on an adventure, a hike, ice skating, or to a football game — make them this hot lunch to take along. Fill a large thermos with hot chili & chopped onions—then tie thread or dental floss around cooked hot dogs & push them down into the chili — leave the strings out. Send along a little bag of buns & napkins. ♥

Christmas: make cookies together to leave for Santa. Tie "hay" (grass, weeds, whatever) into a bundle for Rudolph.

Some-Mores: toast a marshmallow (over a fire). Put thin squares of chocolate on a graham cracker; add marshmallow & another cracker.

Sue's Bag'O Buns

94

MAIN
DISHES

"I don't want to make money. I just want to be wonderful."
♥ Marilyn Monroe

Chipped Beef on Toast

Serves Six

My Joe likes his toast cut up—mine has to be torn. Such is the "Mom food" mystique—all tied up with childhood memories.♥

10 oz. dried beef   6 Tbsp. flour
6 Tbsp. sweet butter   4 c. hot milk
1 c. onion, minced   freshly ground pepper
12 slices hearty white bread, toasted

Pour boiling water over beef—let sit 10 min. Rinse, drain & pat dry. (Removes excess salt.) Melt butter in lg. saucepan, add onions & cook slowly till tender. Sprinkle in flour & whisk for 1 minute. Slowly whisk in hot milk, stirring till it thickens. Add beef & pepper to taste; heat through. Serve over toast. ♥

Macaroni & Cheese

375° Six Servings

10 oz. elbow macaroni   ½ tsp. salt
2 eggs   ¼ tsp. pepper
1 Tbsp. dry mustard   2 c. half & half
1 lb. sharp cheddar cheese, grated

Preheat oven to 375°. Cook & drain the macaroni. In a large bowl, lightly beat eggs with mustard, salt & pepper. Stir in half & half, then the cheese & then cooked macaroni. Pour into a buttered 2 qt. casserole & bake 25 min. Put it under the broiler 1 minute to make the top brown & a little crisp. ♥

More Mom Food:

Scalloped Potatoes with Sausages

350° Serves Four

½ lb. breakfast link sausages
4 c. peeled baking potatoes, sliced
½ lg. onion, thinly sliced
salt & pepper

4 Tbsp. butter
4 Tbsp. flour
3 c. hot milk

Brown sausages well; drain on paper towels. Heat oven to 350°. Slice the potatoes very thinly & separate the onion slices into rings. In a buttered 8"x10" baking pan, layer potatoes with onion rings, sprinkling each layer with salt & pepper. In a lg. saucepan, melt butter; whisk in flour; cook briefly. Slowly whisk in hot milk. Pour over potatoes. Cover tightly with foil; bake 1 hour. Remove foil ~ arrange sausages on top & bake, uncovered, 15 minutes more or until potatoes are tender. ♥

Stuffed Bell Peppers

Preheat oven to 350° Serves Six

6 lg. green peppers
1 lg. onion, chopped
2 ribs celery, diced
3 cloves garlic, minced
2 Tbsp. olive oil
1½ lb. lean ground beef
⅓ c. tomato paste

1 35-oz. can whole tomatoes, drained & chopped
¼ c. parsley, minced
2 tsp. oregano
3 tsp. basil
¼ tsp. red pepper flakes
1 tsp. Worcestershire sauce

½ lb. sharp cheddar, in ½" cubes

Halve peppers lengthwise; remove seeds & membranes. Blanch in boiling water 2 min.; drain. In lg. skillet, sauté onion, celery, & garlic 5 min. Add beef & brown; stir in remaining ingredients. Fill peppers, place on oiled cookie sheet; bake 30 min. Serve. ♥

LEMON NOODLES

400°   Serves Eight

Perfect with fish, but that's not all ~ this stuff is delicious ~ one of my mainstays! Make it all ~ if there's any left over you're going to want it ♥.

1 lb. spaghetti
1/4 lb. butter
1 pt. sour cream
juice of one juicy lemon

1 tsp. grated lemon peel
freshly ground pepper
1/4 c. minced parsley
Parmesan cheese, to taste

Preheat oven to 400°. Cook the noodles in boiling water; drain & put in baking dish. Melt butter in a small saucepan; remove from heat. Stir in sour cream, lemon juice & lemon peel. Pour over pasta, toss & bake 20~25 minutes. Remove from oven, sprinkle on lots of freshly ground pepper, minced parsley & Parmesan cheese. Toss & eat ♥.

"Great art is as irrational as great music.
It is mad with its own loveliness."
♥ George Jean Nathan

ANGEL HAIR and SHRIMP

Serves Two

This is one of those recipes you never really have to measure — just do it to your own taste & make it for as many as you need to feed.

6 extra-large shrimp
angel hair pasta, 1/4 lb.
1 clove garlic, minced
2 Tbsp. olive oil

1 Tbsp. fresh basil, minced
1 c. tomato, chopped
salt & freshly ground
  pepper, to taste

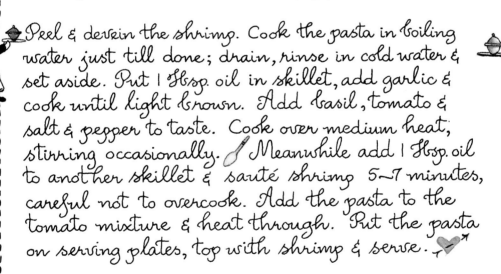

Peel & devein the shrimp. Cook the pasta in boiling water just till done; drain, rinse in cold water & set aside. Put 1 Tbsp. oil in skillet, add garlic & cook until light brown. Add basil, tomato & salt & pepper to taste. Cook over medium heat, stirring occasionally. Meanwhile add 1 Tbsp. oil to another skillet & sauté shrimp 5~7 minutes, careful not to overcook. Add the pasta to the tomato mixture & heat through. Put the pasta on serving plates, top with shrimp & serve.

"Three may keep a secret, if two
of them are dead."
            Benjamin Franklin

LINGUINI AND GRILLED SAUSAGES

Serves Four

I have to thank my high school friend Michael J. Ferejohn, professor of philosophy; cook extraordinaire, for this easy & different pasta dish ♥.

2~3 sausages per person
1 c. black olives, pitted
½ c. chopped parsley
4 anchovy fillets
¼ c. white wine
½ lb. lg. white mushrooms

olive oil
2/3 lb. linguini
3 Tbsp. butter
juice of 1 lemon
Parmesan cheese

Use your favorite kind of sausage, or better yet, try 2 or 3 different kinds. Put them on the grill or brown them in a skillet. Put water on to boil for pasta. Put olives, parsley & anchovies into blender or food processor & chop finely. Add wine & set aside. Thinly slice the mushrooms. Heat a small amount of oil in large skillet to very hot. Add mushrooms & cook quickly over hot flame to seal juices. Start cooking the pasta; drain when done. When mushrooms are crisp, lower heat, add the butter, then the olive/wine mixture —heat through, but don't cook. Remove from heat, add lemon juice & toss with cooked pasta. Add Parmesan cheese to taste & serve with sausages. ♥ Try this with heated French-bread rolls & some good mustard. ♥

SPARERIBS & JUICE ♥

275° Serves Four

My mom called us "wild Indians" sometimes, & never did we look the part more than when we were devouring her wonderful spareribs & juice. She has a picture of us all around the table during one of these feasts ~ my poor dad has a look on his face that clearly says "Must you take a picture NOW?" But the rest of us are smiling, with enough "juice" on our faces, hands & clothes to make a whole other dinner. This was an often-requested birthday dinner & was served with garden corn on the cob dripping with butter & fluffy mashed potatoes WITH lumps. For dessert ~ watermelon ~ served curbside ♥.

Pork ribs for four
2 c. pineapple juice
½ c. catsup
2 Tbsp. steak sauce
2 Tbsp. brown sugar
1 Tbsp. white vinegar
1 tsp. ground mustard
3 cloves minced garlic (opt.)

Put the ribs in a roasting pan & into a 275° oven for 2 hours. Pour off fat. Mix together all remaining ingredients & pour over the ribs. Bake 1 hour more. Serve in a large bowl surrounded with juice. ♥

SOFT~SHELL CRABS

I cannot fathom WHY, in some restaurants, this delicacy is served mushy — it's so easy to make them crisp & delicious. ♥ You can buy them frozen (already cleaned) & eat them whole.

soft~shell crabs ~ 2 to 3 per person
sprigs of fresh thyme (opt.)
flour for dredging
cooking oil ~ ¼"
chopped parsley
lemon wedges

Thaw, rinse & dry the crabs. Tuck a tiny sprig of thyme under the shell of each crab (if you like). Dredge them in flour. Heat the oil in a large skillet — you'll want it very hot — put the crabs in the pan (don't crowd them) & fry hot & fast, about 5 minutes, till brown & crisp. Serve with a sprinkle of parsley & the lemon wedges. ♥

"Who's your fat friend?" (Of George, Prince of Wales.) ♥ "Beau" Brummell

Border text (clockwise from top): home pell mell. Cook him up — fast and hot — eat him quick, on the spot. Bring me a crab that's fat and light — no shell on him to pick tonight. Nab a crab without his shell ~ run the creature

STEAMED CLAMS

Makes 4 dozen

This can be a lovely light summer dinner served with a salad & some French bread. ♥

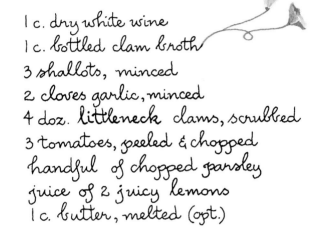

1 c. dry white wine
1 c. bottled clam broth
3 shallots, minced
2 cloves garlic, minced
4 doz. littleneck clams, scrubbed
3 tomatoes, peeled & chopped
handful of chopped parsley
juice of 2 juicy lemons
1 c. butter, melted (opt.)

Combine the wine, broth, shallots & garlic in a large soup pot; bring to boil; add clams. Cover & steam just till they open. Dip the tomatoes in boiling water for 15 seconds — skin will slip off. Chop them finely. Put clams in serving bowl; sprinkle over tomatoes, parsley, & lemon juice. Serve with melted butter for dipping if you like ♥.

"And you shall wander hand in
hand with love in summer's
    wonderland;
Go down to Kew in lilac-time
(it isn't far from London!)"
            ♥ Alfred Noyes

SESAME NOODLES
CHIEN NOIR

Serves Six

The Black Dog Tavern on Martha's Vineyard serves many wonderful dishes, but this has to be my all-time favorite ♥ Thank you, Charlie Esposito!

¼ c. tahini
¼ c. warm water
¼ c. soy sauce (or tamari)
¼ c. vegetable oil
2 Tbsp. sugar

2 Tbsp. cider vinegar
2 cloves garlic, minced
1½ Tbsp. chili oil
2 tsp. sesame oil
½ c. green onions
16 oz. thin udon noodles

Look for any unfamiliar ingredients at your health food store. Whisk together tahini & warm water; whisk in soy sauce, vegetable oil, sugar, vinegar, garlic, chili oil & sesame oil. Finely chop green onions. Cook the noodles according to package; lightly coat them with sauce, tossing gently. Sprinkle on green onions & serve. ♥ Best hot or at room temperature. Try Chinese egg noodles if you can't find the udon. ♥

" My little old dog: A heart-beat at my feet."
♥ Edith Wharton

CHICKEN IN CHERRY SAUCE

Serves Six

♥ A special company dinner—an old recipe from home.

1 med. onion, minced | more butter
2 Tbsp. butter | 1 can pitted dark cherries
2 Tbsp. oil | 3 Tbsp. cornstarch
4 whole, boned & skinned chicken | 2 c. chicken stock
   breasts, halved | ¼ c. sherry

flour for dredging, mixed with salt & pepper

♥ Preheat oven to 200° Slowly sauté onion in butter & oil, about 15 min. Remove onion from pan with slotted spoon & reserve. Pound chicken breasts to achieve uniform thickness, dredge in flour. Add more butter to skillet, making 4 Tbsp. Cook breasts, in batches, 2-3 min. each side, till just cooked through. Remove to platter & keep in warm oven. Drain cherries; reserve juice. Combine juice, cornstarch & stock—pour into the hot skillet & scrape up bits in pan. Boil 3 min.; add reserved onions, cherries & sherry. Heat through. Pour some sauce over the chicken breasts & pass the rest in a sauceboat. ♥

"Father, I cannot tell a lie. I did it with my little hatchet."
♥ George Washington

Sun-Dried
TOMATO PESTO

Makes 1 cup; serves four

Quick & easy — all the good things: garlic, sun-dried tomatoes, Parmesan cheese, herbs . . . all together to make this delicious spicy pasta sauce. ♥

1/4 c. almonds, chopped
4~6 oz. sun-dried tomatoes, with oil
1/2 c. olive oil
1/4 c. grated Parmesan cheese
1 Tbsp. garlic, minced
1 Tbsp. onion, minced

1/2 tsp. oregano
1/2 tsp. basil
1/4 tsp. thyme
dash of red pepper
flakes
2 Tbsp. lemon juice

Everything goes into the food processor — whirl till you have a thick, grainy sauce. Cover and refrigerate, or serve immediately: 1/4 c. on each serving of pasta. Pass some additional Parmesan & enjoy. ♥

"I know I have the body of a weak and feeble woman, but I have the heart and stomach of a king, and of a king of England too. . . ."
♥ Queen Elizabeth I

CHICKEN IN PHYLLO

400° Serves Four

Cut into these & out comes the melted cheese. ♥

2 whole, boned, skinned chicken breasts
1 stick butter, melted
1 pkg. phyllo
4 Tbsp. shallots, minced
1 tsp. sage
4 oz. jack cheese

Preheat oven to 400°. Halve chicken breasts & pound flat. Melt butter. Layer 4 sheets phyllo, buttering each sheet. On each chicken breast sprinkle 1 Tbsp. shallots & ¼ tsp. sage. Lay 1 oz. cheese on each breast & roll up. Place breast in the middle of the phyllo, at one end; roll once, fold in sides, brush with butter & continue rolling, buttering as you go. Lay all on ungreased cookie sheet & bake 25 min., till browned. Serve. ♥

The Leader of the Pack

"If a recipe cannot be written on the face of a 3×5 card, off with its head."
♥ Helen Nearing

(Not Just the Regular)
STEW

Made with good-quality beef, fresh vegetables, red wine, & herbs; served with hot crusty French bread, a dry red wine & a crisp salad — it's perfect for a frosty night at home. ♥

2 lbs. tenderloin, cut in 1-inch cubes

flour for dredging

2 tbsp. each butter & oil

2 cloves garlic, minced

salt & freshly ground pepper

2 c. dry red wine

2 beef bouillon cubes dissolved in 2 c. boiling water

1 baking potato, grated

1 onion, peeled & studded with 2 cloves

2 tsp. thyme

1 bay leaf

8 red potatoes, unpeeled & quartered

8 carrots, sliced

4 stalks celery, sliced

8 tiny white onions

1 or 2 c. tomato juice

handful of fresh parsley, finely chopped

Dredge meat in flour. Melt butter & oil in large pot; add garlic. Cook the beef just to rare; remove from pot & refrigerate. Add wine & bouillon to pan & scrape up bits stuck to bottom. Add potato, onion, thyme & bay leaf. Bring to boil, cover & simmer 1 hour. Add potatoes, carrots, celery & onions; simmer ½ hr. Add tomato juice, as necessary for nice gravy. Add beef cubes, reheat; toss in parsley & serve. ♥

CHICKEN &
DUMPLINGS

Serves Six

My grandmother is one of 10 children & grew up in that peaceful time before T.V. & radio ♥. On Sundays, after church, they would gather in the 3rd floor music room of their Iowa home to sing & be musical ♪. Afterwards they'd sit down to a big chicken dinner "with all the fixin's." Chicken & Dumplings was a favorite. ♥

8 pieces chicken (about 5 lb.)
3 ribs celery, sliced
4 carrots, sliced
1 lg. onion, chopped
freshly ground pepper
2 tsp. salt
2 Tbsp. parsley, minced
2 tsp. thyme

½ tsp. rosemary

2 c. unbleached flour
1 tsp. salt
3 tsp. baking powder
2 Tbsp. parsley, minced
¼ c. shortening (Crisco)
¾ c. whole milk

Wash & dry the chicken. In a large pot, brown the pieces in a little oil. Put in the vegetables & herbs; add water to cover & bring to a boil. Reduce heat & simmer 20 min. Meanwhile, make the dumplings. Combine flour, salt, baking powder & parsley. With pastry cutter, cut in the shortening till it resembles coarse meal. Stir in milk with a fork just to make dough hold together. Drop the dough onto simmering broth, by tablespoonfuls. Cover & continue simmering 20 min. more without peeking. To serve, put chicken piece in a wide soup bowl with dumplings & ladle over hot broth. ♥

"It is a great art to saunter."
♥ Henry David Thoreau

VEAL WITH DUMPLINGS

375°   Serves Eight

Yes, there's canned soup in this — but I don't care — it's GOOD. It's also the dish I requested for my birthday dinners (Ultimate Mom Food ♥.)

Veal

2 lb. veal cutlets, cut in 1" pieces
flour
4 Tbsp. butter
salt & pepper
1 c. water

1 lg. onion, sliced
2 Tbsp. butter
1 can cream of chicken soup
1 3/4 c. water

   Roll veal in flour & brown quickly in butter. Add salt, pepper, & water; simmer 30 min. Meanwhile, in another pan, slowly cook onion in butter. Pour the veal into a 9"x13" casserole; arrange onion on top. In the veal skillet, bring the soup & water to a boil & pour over veal. Make the

Dumplings

2 c. flour
4 tsp. baking powder
1/2 tsp. salt
1 tsp. poultry seasoning

1 Tbsp. poppy seeds
1/4 c. salad oil
1 c. milk
3 Tbsp. melted butter
3/4 c. bread crumbs

   Preheat oven to 375°. Mix together first 5 ingredients. Stir in oil & milk. Mix melted butter & bread crumbs — roll rounded tablespoons of batter into bread crumb mixture and place on top of veal. Bake 20 min.

Sauce (which, believe it or not, is delicious!)

1 c. sour cream
1 c. cream of chicken soup

Combine & heat. Pass separately to be poured over dumplings & veal ♥.

STEAK AU POIVRE

Serves Two

Devil food ~ so good & so bad! But outrageously delicious ♥

1–1½ Tbsp. cracked black peppercorns
2 tenderloin steaks, at least 1¼" thick
2 Tbsp. butter
1 Tbsp. shallots, minced

2 Tbsp. cognac
2 Tbsp. red wine
¼ c. beef broth
2 Tbsp. heavy cream

Crack the peppercorns in mortar & pestle or with rolling pin on board. Press them into steaks. Heat butter in heavy skillet. Sear steaks over med. high heat, both sides, turning with tongs. Reduce heat to med. & cook, turning often, till desired doneness. Remove meat from pan & keep warm. Add shallots to pan & sauté a minute or so. Add cognac & wine — boil 2 min., stirring. Add beef broth & boil 2 more min., scraping up bits from pan. Stir in cream, heat through but don't boil. Pour sauce over steaks & serve. ♥

VICTIM LEAVING TOWN

MIXED SHELLFISH

400°

This elegant dish takes only minutes to prepare. ♥

For each serving:

> 2 jumbo shrimp, peeled & cleaned
> 6 tiny scallops, or 2 large,
>   cut in bite-sized pieces
> 4 pieces cooked lobster meat
> 1 Tbsp. shallots, minced
> 1 Tbsp. parsley, minced
> olive oil
> dry vermouth
> lemon wedge

Preheat oven to 400°. Put the fish into a shell dish. Sprinkle on shallots & parsley; dribble over a little olive oil & a splash of vermouth. Bake about 10 min. Serve with lemon wedge. ♥ Be very careful not to overcook. ♥

A recipe for fish baked in ashes: "No cheese, no nonsense! Just place it tenderly in fig leaves and tie them on top with a string; then push it under hot ashes, bethinking thee wisely of the time when it is done, and burn it not up." ♥ Archestratus, 4th century B. C.

SOLE MEUNIÈRE

Serves Four

Your basic fabulous fish dish ♥

2 lb. sole fillets, very fresh
unbleached flour
2 tbsp. vegetable oil
6 tbsp. butter
¼ c. minced parsley
juice of 1 juicy lemon

Rinse the sole & pat dry. Dredge in flour to coat; shake off excess. Heat oil plus 2 tbsp. butter in skillet till hot. Brown fillets quickly, turning once. Remove to warm platter. Add re~ maining butter to skillet; when it begins to bubble, scrape up brown bits in pan & remove from heat. Stir in parsley & lemon juice. Pour over fillets & serve at once. ♥

"Everything that lives in water is seductive." ♥   Jean~Paul Aron

DUCK À L'ORANGE

375° Serves Two, maybe Three

Easy to do—if it's for a special evening, get some paper frills for the legs—duck ankles are notoriously thin.

a 5~6 lb. duck
2 oranges
1 lemon
3 Tbsp. red wine vinegar
1 Tbsp. sugar
2 Tbsp. brandy
1/4 c. hot chicken stock
thin orange & lemon slices, for garnish

Roast the duck in preheated 375° oven, on a rack, for 20~25 min. per pound. Prick the skin several times to release fat & baste every 15 min. Meanwhile, grate the rind of the oranges & lemon; blanch in boiling water 20 seconds; drain; set aside. On a small saucepan, simmer vinegar & sugar till sugar melts, turns a little brown & thickens slightly. Add the juice of the oranges & the lemon; simmer briefly & add the blanched rinds. When duck is done, remove to hot platter & decorate with orange & lemon slices (paper frills for duck ankles, if desired). Allow duck to sit 15 min. before carving. From duck pan, pour off all fat, leaving only the brown juices. Over high heat, add brandy & chicken stock, scraping brown bits from pan; pour into orange sauce. Reheat & serve in a sauceboat.

PIZZA

This is made with real French bread & you'll have enough dough here for four 10" pies. Eat 1, freeze 3, & you'll always be ready for the craving you're sure to have from now on. ♥

Bread

1 pkg. dry yeast
2 c. lukewarm water
2 tsp. salt

1 Tbsp. sugar
4~5 c. flour
olive oil

Dissolve yeast in water. Let stand 5 min. Stir in salt & sugar. Gradually mix in the flour, till it won't take anymore. Knead on floured board 3~4 min. Let rise 1 hr. in greased bowl, covered, in a warm spot. Punch down, divide into four pieces. Wrap 3 separately & freeze. Stretch remaining piece into 10 inch round. Put on buttered baking sheet & let rise, covered, 45 min. Brush with olive oil. Bake at 400° for 12~15 min. with a pan of boiling water on lower rack. ♥

Filling

1½ broccoli, cut small
1~2 tomatoes, sliced
1 clove garlic, minced
½ tsp. oregano
½ tsp. rosemary
½ tsp. basil

sprinkle of red pepper flakes
5 sun-dried tomatoes, chopped
4 oz. brie, thinly sliced
8 kalamata olives, chopped
Parmesan cheese
freshly ground pepper

Steam broccoli till tender. Put tomatoes on baked pie, then broccoli, & rest of ingredients in order. Broil till cheese melts. Serve ♥. Any group of ingredients that sounds good to you, please try. In the summer try tomatoes with lots of fresh basil & Montrachet cheese. ♥

Little Dinners

My own tastes lean away from the "main dish" & more toward the "little dinner" ~ combinations of soups, salads & vegetable dishes. So here are a few of my favorite recipes for little dinners. ♥

Welsh Rabbit

Serves Two

½ lb. sharp cheddar, diced   dash cayenne
1 Tbsp. butter   1 egg, slightly beaten
½ tsp. dry mustard   ½ c. beer
¼ tsp. Worcestershire sauce   4 slices hearty white
                                   bread, toasted

Melt cheese & butter in top of double boiler over boiling water. Stirring constantly, add mustard, Worcestershire, & cayenne. Beat in egg; stir in beer, & stir till hot. Do not boil. Serve over toast. ♥

Vegetable Quesadillas

For each person: melt a pat of butter in a large skillet over med. heat. Lay a flour tortilla in pan; cover with thinly sliced jack cheese; then sprinkle over a combination of tomatoes, olives, red onion & green pepper, all diced. Put another tortilla on top. Cover pan & cook till cheese is almost melted; carefully flip tortillas & cook other side. Cut it like a pie & serve it with salsa (p.25) & sour cream. ♥

Little Dinners:

" In giving a dinner, the error is usually on the side of abundance." Thomas Cooper

Rice & Vegetables

For each person: Put about 3/4 c. cooked brown rice in an ovenproof dish. Top with: chopped tomato, grated carrot, finely chopped broccoli, minced green onion, minced parsley, toasted pine nuts, freshly ground pepper — and any other vegetables & herbs you like. Spread grated jack or Muenster cheese over the top. Bake at 350° for 1/2 hour. ♥

Beans & Rice

Serves Two

1 can beans
2 c. cooked brown rice
3 tbsp. chopped onion

garnishes, opt.:
sour cream
salsa

Get health food store beans — refried, or what you like; heat them up. Put hot rice on plate, cover with beans, sprinkle over onions. If you like, add a dollop of sour cream & a spoonful of salsa. ♥

Pita Bread Sandwich

Into food processor put cooked chicken, lots of different raw vegetables & herbs, a squeeze of lemon juice, a bit of mustard. Whirl to the consistency of rice. Pile into toasted whole wheat pita bread. ♥

Romance:

A beautiful word that even sounds pretty. And that's what romance is all about — it's a celebration of the senses. ♥ Things that taste, smell, feel, sound, & look wonderful are the stuff romance is made of. It's the celebration of being Alive. If you want a special & romantic time, try to appeal to the 5 senses, throw in a little imagination, and voilà!

A few ideas:

When you and your husband (PAL, FRIEND?) go on vacation, wire ahead for flowers & champagne to be waiting in your room. ♥

When it's a car trip, pull out a surprise basket of delights — fruit, cheese, bread & wine. ♥

Plant a romantic garden — an English perennial garden — a traditional herb garden. Use the old-fashioned varieties of flowers — old roses, etc. Plant raspberries. ♥

Do something every year that becomes a tradition. Do sensual food — use crystal & silver, light candles, play appropriate music, have lots of flowers. ♥

Write handwritten letters (not typed) — include photos, cartoons, dried flowers, or quotes. ♥

"Mooshey" beds are romantic — feather pillows, soft comforters, fresh flowered sheets; open nearby windows. ♥

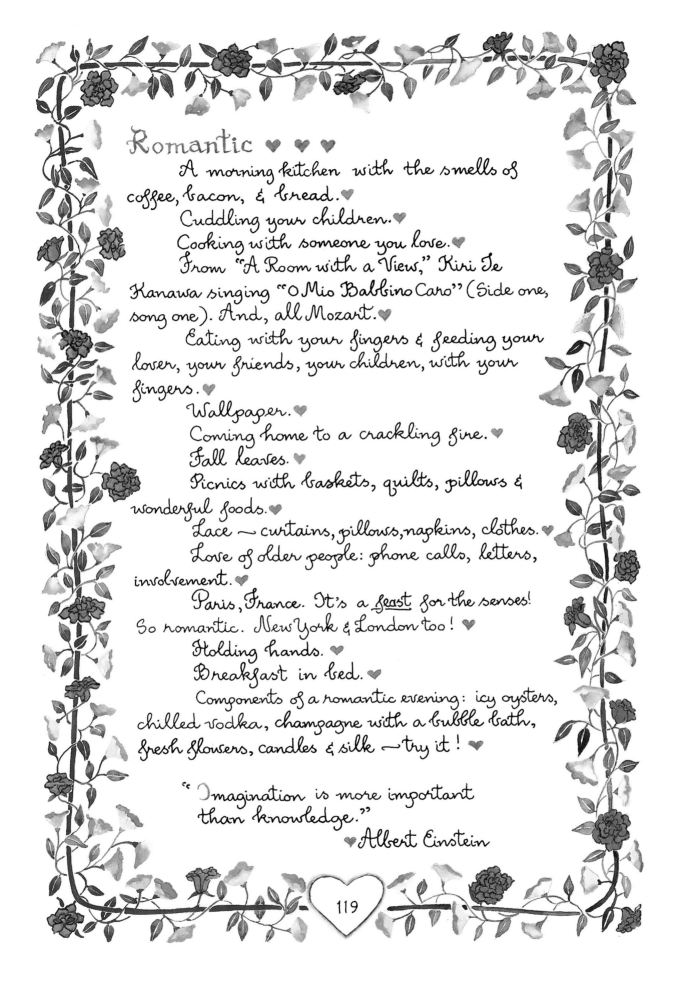

Romantic ♥ ♥ ♥

A morning kitchen with the smells of coffee, bacon, & bread. ♥

Cuddling your children. ♥

Cooking with someone you love. ♥

From "A Room with a View," Kiri Te Kanawa singing "O Mio Babbino Caro" (Side one, song one). And, all Mozart. ♥

Eating with your fingers & feeding your lover, your friends, your children, with your fingers. ♥

Wallpaper. ♥

Coming home to a crackling fire. ♥

Fall leaves. ♥

Picnics with baskets, quilts, pillows & wonderful foods. ♥

Lace — curtains, pillows, napkins, clothes. ♥

Love of older people: phone calls, letters, involvement. ♥

Paris, France. It's a _feast_ for the senses! So romantic. New York & London too! ♥

Holding hands. ♥

Breakfast in bed. ♥

Components of a romantic evening: icy oysters, chilled vodka, champagne with a bubble bath, fresh flowers, candles & silk — try it! ♥

"Imagination is more important
than knowledge."
♥ Albert Einstein

119

"If you cannot inspire a woman with love of you, fill her above the brim with love of herself — all that runs over will be yours."
♥ Charles Caleb Colton

Desserts

Life is Short~
Eat Dessert First

TAPIOCA PUDDING

Serves Eight

Light & delicate—there is something comforting & old-fashioned about this dessert. ♥

4 eggs, separated
3 3/4 c. whole milk
6 Tbsp. quick tapioca
10 Tbsp. sugar
1/4 tsp. salt
2 tsp. vanilla
zest of 1 lemon

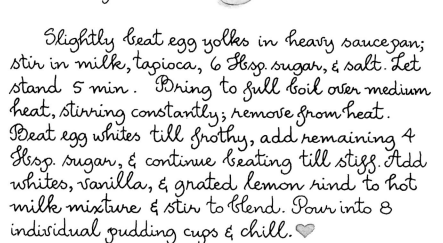

Slightly beat egg yolks in heavy saucepan; stir in milk, tapioca, 6 Tbsp. sugar, & salt. Let stand 5 min. Bring to full boil over medium heat, stirring constantly; remove from heat. Beat egg whites till frothy, add remaining 4 Tbsp. sugar, & continue beating till stiff. Add whites, vanilla, & grated lemon rind to hot milk mixture & stir to blend. Pour into 8 individual pudding cups & chill. ♥

"Across the gateway of my heart
I wrote 'No Thoroughfare,'
But love came laughing by, and cried:
'I enter everywhere.'"
♥ Herbert Shipman

122

LEMON ROLL

375° Serves Ten

A luscious, really beautiful cake — it's so soft & delicate
it reminds me of a newborn baby — you'll see what I mean. ✳
It's easy & it's elegant. ♥

3 eggs, separated	1 tsp. baking powder
1 c. sugar	¼ tsp. salt
6 Tbsp. hot water	grated rind of 1 lemon
1 c. flour	Lemon Filling

powdered sugar

Preheat oven to 375°. Beat egg yolks, add sugar & beat
till thick & lemon-colored. Stir in water & dry ingredients.
Fold in stiffly beaten egg whites. Add grated rind. Grease
a cookie sheet that has a rim (jelly roll pan), line it
with waxed paper & grease it again. Pour batter into
pan, spreading evenly. Bake 12~15 min. Immediately
cut off crisp edges & turn out onto large cloth LIGHTLY covered
with powdered sugar. Remove waxed paper. Using the
cloth, roll up the cake 🔲→ & set aside while you make
the filling. When ready, unroll cake, spread on filling
& roll back up. Cool completely; transfer to serving dish.
Cut with serrated knife ♥.

Lemon Filling

1 c. sugar	Put all ingredients in double
2 eggs	boiler — beat well & stir till
2 Tbsp. butter, melted	thick — 15-20 min. Cool slightly.
juice & grated rind of 2 lemons	♥

Boston Cream Pie

Makes 8 glorious servings

Well, this is my first "two~pager" & I promise you, it's well worth it! I love traditional foods & this is Boston Cream Pie at its most outrageous: creamy & chocolaty, with a light cake ~ 3 heavenly textures in one. ♥

Cream Filling

2 egg yolks
1½ Tbsp. flour
1 Tbsp. cornstarch
¼ c. powdered sugar

1½ c. whole milk
1 Tbsp. butter
½ c. whipping cream
1 tsp. vanilla

Beat the yolks in a double boiler; stir in flour, cornstarch, sugar, milk & butter. Cook over boiling water about 20 min. till thick, stirring constantly. Chill mixture. When cold, whip the cream with the vanilla & fold together. Refrigerate. ♥

Sponge Cake

3 eggs, separated
¼ c. cold water
3/4 c. sugar
½ tsp. vanilla
¼ tsp. lemon zest

3/4 c. cake flour
¼ tsp. baking powder
⅛ tsp. salt
½ tsp. cream of tartar

Preheat oven to 325°. Separate eggs ~ yolks into lg. bowl, whites into smaller 🥛. Beat the yolks for 5 min.;

Continued...

      gradually add cold water & beat 1 minute. Add sugar gradually & beat 3 more minutes. Stir in vanilla & lemon zest. In another bowl, mix together flour, baking powder & salt with a fork. Add to yolk mixture in thirds, folding in. Beat the whites with the cream of tartar till they form soft peaks. Fold into yolk mixture. Turn into 2 ungreased 8" cake pans. Bake at 325° for 15~20 min. till golden & springs back to touch. Cool upside down. Run a sharp knife around outside & remove cakes from pan. Refrigerate. When ready to frost (when cream & cake are chilled) make the

Chocolate Icing

2 squares unsweetened chocolate (2 oz)	1 egg yolk
3/4 c. powdered sugar	3 Tbsp. cream
1 Tbsp. water	½ tsp. vanilla

    Melt chocolate in top of double boiler, remove from heat. Beat in sugar & water at once. Add yolk, beat well. Beat in cream, 1 Tbsp. at a time, then vanilla ♥.

Ta~Daa...

    Put the cream filling between cake layers. Spread the chocolate over the top, allowing some to dribble over edges. Keep cake refrigerated. ♥

STRAWBERRY SHORTCAKE

400° Serves Eight

The old-fashioned kind, like Mom used to make ♥.

4 c. unbleached flour
½ c. sugar
2 Tbsp. baking powder
¼ tsp. salt
½ c. butter

1 beaten egg
1¼ c. whole milk
3 c. heavy cream
5 c. strawberries

Wash, hull & halve the berries. Put them in a glass bowl & sprinkle 2 or 3 Tbsp. sugar over. Cover & chill. Turn oven to 400°. Combine first 4 ingredients. Chop butter into pieces & cut into flour mixture till crumbly. Beat in egg & milk. Butter 2 baking sheets. Using ½ c. dough per "biscuit," make 8 4" rounds. Bake 15~17 min. till golden. Whip the cream, adding sugar to taste. Put berries on top of shortcake, then a big dollop of whipped cream. ♥ Best served when short~ cake is warm; you can reheat them. ♥ The berries will be juicier if you crush a few before sugaring & let them sit for an hour before using. ♥

Truffles

Makes about 40

A wonderful gift for Christmas or Valentine's Day; truffles are quick & easy to make. Make your after-dinner coffee more special by serving these melt-in-your-mouth chocolate morsels alongside. ♥

6 oz. semi-sweet chocolate
2 egg yolks
2/3 c. unsalted butter, softened
1 1/3 c. powdered sugar, sifted
2 tsp. vanilla
1/2 c. walnuts, chopped
unsweetened cocoa powder
2 tsp. crème de menthe or Grand Marnier (opt.)

Over very low heat, slowly melt chocolate in a small saucepan, stirring often. Remove from heat & cool. Cream egg yolks & butter together. Add sugar slowly & blend well. Pour the cooled chocolate into sugar mixture; add vanilla & nuts. Stir. (If using a liqueur, omit vanilla & substitute liqueur.) Refrigerate until firm enough to handle. Shape into 1" balls; roll in cocoa; chill. Keep refrigerated till ready to serve. Can be frozen. ♥

ORANGE CAKE

Serves 8~10

To die for. ♥ A real special-occasion cake perfect for spring teas, Mother's Day, showers or a pre~wedding party. ♥

Orange Filling

6 Tbsp. sugar
1½ Tbsp. cornstarch
pinch of salt
½ c. water

½ tsp. grated orange peel
½ c. fresh orange juice
1 egg yolk, slightly beaten
1 Tbsp. butter, melted

½ c. crushed pineapple

In top part of double boiler, over boiling water, mix sugar, cornstarch & salt. Gradually add water, orange peel & juice, then egg yolk. Cook, stirring, till smooth & thick. Fold in butter & pineapple. Chill ♥.

The Cake

4 Tbsp. butter
1 c. sugar
2 eggs, separated

1½ c. flour
2 tsp. baking powder
pinch of salt

½ c. fresh orange juice

Preheat oven to 350°. Cream butter & sugar. Add egg yolks & beat till thick & lemon-colored. With a fork, mix together dry ingredients & add them alternately with the o.j. Fold in stiffly beaten egg whites. Pour into two buttered 8" cake pans & bake at 350° for 20 minutes. Cool completely & remove from pans. ♥

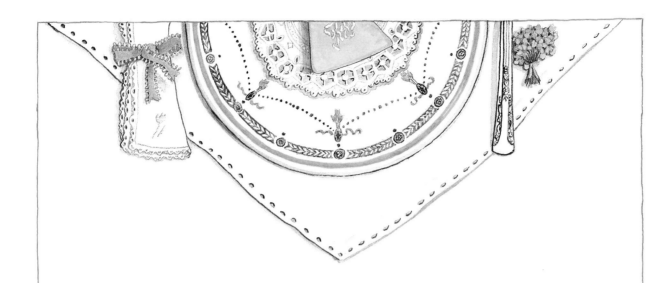

Orange Icing

zest of 1 orange   1½ c. powdered sugar
juice of 1 orange   1 tsp. white rum
       coconut for garnish (opt.)

Lightly grate rind of orange & bring it & the juice to a boil. Strain the juice & pour as much hot juice over sugar as needed to make right consistency for spreading. Stir in rum. ♥

To Assemble

Put the chilled filling between layers. Frost with orange icing, allowing some to dribble over edges. Sprinkle on coconut if you like. The cake looks beautiful served on plates lined with lace doilies. ♥

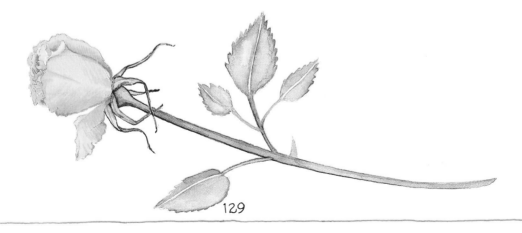

129

CHOCOLATE CAKE

350° Serves Eight

If you like a rich, dense, fudge-like cake with a texture almost like creamy peanut butter, this is the recipe for you ♥. Notice that it calls for no flour. ♥

16 oz. semi-sweet chocolate
1 c. unsalted butter
9 eggs, separated

1 c. sugar
unsweetened cocoa or
flour, for dusting

Preheat oven to 350°. Butter a 9" springform pan; line the bottom with buttered wax paper; dust pan with cocoa or flour. Slowly melt chocolate & butter together in a heavy saucepan over low heat; cool. Meanwhile separate eggs into two large bowls. Beat the yolks for about a minute; slowly add sugar & continue beating till thick & lemon-colored. Beat egg whites until they just begin to peak. Add cooled chocolate mixture to egg yolks & blend thoroughly. Pour the chocolate & yolk mixture into egg whites & fold gently until completely blended. Remove 1/3 of the batter to refrigerator & cover. Pour rest of batter into prepared pan & bake 40-45 minutes. Cool 1/2 hour before turning out onto serving plate. Frost with remaining batter. Garnishes include whipped cream, sliced almonds, sifted powdered sugar; all are optional. ♥ For Valentine's Day: cut out another round of wax paper & draw hearts on it; cut them out. Lay the paper on cake & sift powdered sugar over the top. Remove paper carefully. ♥

FUDGE

This recipe always comes out perfectly & without the use of a candy thermometer. Give it to someone special on Valentine's Day ~ it's a must at Christmastime ♥.

1 lg. can condensed milk
4 c. sugar
16 oz. semi~sweet chocolate bits

½ lb. sweet butter
chopped nuts of choice (opt)

Put the milk & sugar in a heavy pan. Bring to a boil. Start timing when boiling starts ~ cook 8½ minutes, stirring constantly. Put the chocolate bits & butter in a large bowl & pour the sugar mixture over. Mix with electric mixer, blending well. Stir in chopped nuts & spread in buttered pan to a depth of 1 inch. Partially chill & cut in squares with a hot knife. Refrigerate. ♥

"I wasn't kissing her, I was whispering in her mouth."
♥ Chico Marx

ALMOND BRITTLE

This makes a perfect candy for gift giving—especially good for mailing. But it comes with a warning: make it, get it packed, & get it OUT of the house. Sometimes I let it sit out cooling too long & somehow it's GONE before I get it sent. (DON'T LOOK AT ME ☺) ♥

You will need a candy thermometer for this.
2 c. sugar
1 lb. unsalted (sweet) butter
¼ c. water
10 oz. sliced almonds
8 oz. unsweetened chocolate

Combine sugar, butter, & water in large heavy pot. Stirring constantly, bring to a boil over moderately high heat. Occasionally dip a pastry brush in cold water & wash down sugar from sides of pan. Boil rapidly, stirring, till temperature reaches 295°. Remove from heat. Quickly stir in almonds & spread thinly on 2 cookie sheets. Melt the chocolate over very low heat. When candy is just slightly warm, almost cool, brush with melted chocolate. When chocolate has hardened, break into pieces & store in an airtight container. ♥

"Never eat more than you can lift."
🐷 Miss Piggy

INDIAN PUDDING

300° Serves Eight

An old New England favorite, this pudding is best served warm with a big scoop of vanilla ice cream. It's a comforting wintertime dessert. ♥

5½ c. whole milk   1 tsp. ginger
2/3 c. cornmeal   1 tsp. cinnamon
4 Tbsp. butter   ½ tsp. salt
½ c. maple syrup   1 c. raisins
¼ c. molasses   vanilla ice cream

Preheat oven to 300°. Butter a small casserole ~ mine is 6½" x 10½". Over med. heat, in a large saucepan, heat the milk but don't boil it. Slowly whisk in cornmeal & continue to stir until mixture begins to thicken ~ 10 min. or so. Add remaining ingredients & keep stirring till heated through. Pour into casserole & bake 3 hours till sides are brown & sticky-looking. (The pudding hardens a bit as it cools.) Serve warm with vanilla ice cream. ♥

"No Spring, nor Summer Beauty
     hath such grace,
As I have seen in one Autumnall face."
          ♥ John Donne

BOURBON BALLS

Makes about 60

A delicious holiday candy. 🖤

1 box powdered sugar, plus ⅓ c.	4 oz. unsweetened chocolate
1 stick butter, softened	1 oz. paraffin wax, grated
⅓ c. bourbon	1 box toothpicks

Sift 1 box powdered sugar over butter & cream together thoroughly. Stir in bourbon & put into freezer 5 min. Sift the ⅓ c. powdered sugar onto plate. Roll sugar mixture into 1" balls, then in powdered sugar. Place them onto cookie sheet & into freezer for 15 min. Stick a toothpick into each ball. Melt chocolate & paraffin together. Working quickly, dip each ball in chocolate; place on wax paper on cookie sheet. Remove picks. Reheat chocolate, then dribble a bit more on each candy to cover toothpick hole. Put them back in freezer 5 more min. Store in covered container in refrigerator. 🖤

"Lost, yesterday, somewhere between sunrise and sunset, two golden hours, each set with sixty diamond minutes. No reward is offered, for they are gone forever."
🖤 Horace Mann

OLD-FASHIONED APPLE PIE

450° Serves Eight

This is the kind of country pie they used to make in the "good old days" — with a tall top crust filled with juicy apples.

14 green apples, peeled, cored & sliced
1 c. brown sugar
1 tsp. cinnamon
½ tsp. nutmeg

¼ tsp. salt
3½ Tbsp. cornstarch
1 Tbsp. lemon juice
2 Tbsp. butter

Combine all ingredients except butter. Pour into pie shell, piling high in the middle. Dot with butter. Cover with top crust. Cut out vents in top center. Bake on cookie sheet 10 min. at 450°, reduce heat to 350° & bake 40~50 min. longer till apples are tender & crust is brown. ♥

Pie Crust

4 c. unbleached flour
2 tsp. salt

2 c. Crisco shortening
ice water to form ball

♥ Chill all ingredients ~ 1 hr.

Put the flour & salt in a bowl & cut in Crisco with pastry cutter to the size of small peas. Slowly add ice water, stirring with fork till dough comfortably holds together in a ball. Flour a board & rolling pin. You'll need a bottom crust ⅛" thick & about 10" in diameter & a top crust of at least 16" in diameter. Divide dough accordingly & roll out bottom crust; put into 8" pie dish. Fill with apples; lay over top crust, fold & crimp edges. See above to finish. ♥

WITCHES' BREW

Makes 12 cups

This is a holiday brew made by GOOD witches ♥. It's really very elegant & is perfect for Halloween, Thanksgiving & Christmas parties. ♥

1 dozen eggs, separated
2/3 c. milk
1 c. sugar
pinch of salt
1¼ c. whipping cream, whipped

1 46 oz. can apricot nectar
1¼ c. brandy
⅓ c. Triple Sec
nutmeg

In the top part of double boiler, beat egg yolks well. Add the milk, ¾ c. sugar, & salt; cook over simmering water 20 min., stirring occasionally. Cool. Beat the egg whites till frothy, add ¼ c. sugar & continue beating till stiff. Whip the cream & pour into whites; pour cooled custard over all & gently fold till blended. Gently stir in nectar, brandy, & Triple Sec. Cover & refrigerate overnight. When ready to serve, beat it with a whisk, then pour into a punch bowl. Sprinkle with nutmeg & serve. Note: I have a Man-in-the-Moon mold 🌙 I use to make one big ice cube to put in at Halloween, & a star-shaped one for Christmas. It's not necessary, but it helps if the room is warm. ♥

"Nothing can be truer than fairy wisdom. It is as true as sunbeams." ♥ Douglas Jerrold

(Baked Alaska, or)
SNOWBALL IN HELL

450° Serves Six

Individual mountains of meringue covering ice cream & cake, quickly browned & served in a puddle of hot chocolate sauce. Easy! Perfect for Christmas Eve dinner. ♥

Meringue:
- 4 egg whites
- 6 Tbsp. powdered sugar
- pinch of salt
- 1 tsp. vanilla

- 6 1" slices angel food cake
- 6 big scoops vanilla ice cream
- Chocolate Sauce

First make the chocolate sauce. Preheat oven to 450°. Beat egg whites till stiff (not dry). Gradually beat in sugar, then add salt & vanilla. Put parchment paper on rimless cookie sheet. Lay out six slices cake about 3" x 3" each. Working quickly, place a big scoop of ice cream on each slice; spread meringue to cover ice cream & cake, making it look like a mountain 🏔. Bake 3~4 min. till browned. Slide off onto dishes & surround with a puddle of Chocolate Sauce. Serve. ♥

Chocolate Sauce

- 1½ Tbsp. butter
- 2 oz. unsweetened chocolate
- ⅓ c. boiling water

- ¾ c. sugar
- 3 Tbsp. corn syrup
- 1 Tbsp. rum

Melt butter & chocolate in heavy saucepan. Stir in boiling water, then sugar & syrup. Stirring, bring to boil. Boil softly 8-9 min. without stirring. Remove from heat; cool 15 min. Stir in rum. ♥

Orange Ice

Serves Four

Delicious and refreshing on its own, but for gorgeous color & more sophistication try it with Raspberry Sauce (p.139). ♥

3 c. fresh orange juice
½ c. sugar
½ c. lemon juice
grated rind of 2 oranges

Bring orange juice to boil. Stir in sugar till dissolved. Cool. Add lemon juice & rind. Freeze in hand-cranked or electric ice cream maker. You can also freeze it in a metal bowl, stir~ring every so often. Ices are best when served slightly mushy—not frozen stiff. ♥

Tip: The wonderful Donvier ice cream maker makes ice cream & ices in minutes with no electricity & no fuss. Get one. ♥

RASPBERRY SAUCE

Makes 1 cup

Spoon some of this beautiful red sauce onto a
plate & set a scoop of Orange Ice (p.138) on top.
Or try it with a slice of Chocolate Cake (p.130).
Also good with ice cream and/or waffles. ♥

2 c. fresh (or frozen) raspberries
2 Tbsp. currant jelly
1–2 Tbsp. sugar
1 tsp. cornstarch

Crush the raspberries & force through sieve to
remove seeds. Put the raspberry juice, along with
the jelly, into a small saucepan & bring to a boil.
Add sugar to taste; simmer 2 min. Mix the
cornstarch with 1 Tbsp. cold water till smooth;
slowly whisk mixture into sauce. Cook, stirring,
5–7 min. till thickened. Chill. ♥

CHOCOLATE MOUSSE

Serves Eight

I have a chocoholic girl friend out in California who makes all other chocolate lovers pale by comparison. So I knew exactly who to go to when I wanted the most exquisite Chocolate Mousse possible. Very rich & chocolaty but uses no egg yolks as most recipes do. (Diana probably thinks it's diet food ♥.)

8-oz. semisweet chocolate
¼ c. dark rum
½ c. sugar

2-3 Tbsp. lukewarm water
2 egg whites
2 c. heavy cream

Melt chocolate in top of double boiler. Meanwhile cook rum & sugar over very low heat till sugar melts (do not let it brown). Add sugar syrup to chocolate (they should be about the same temp.). Beat in 2 Tbsp. lukewarm water; set aside. Beat egg whites till stiff; whip cream & fold together. Beat chocolate again— if it has thickened, add 1 more Tbsp. water. Fold chocolate into cream & spoon into individual serving dishes or wine glasses. Chill.

SWEET POTATO PIE

475°   Serves Eight

This pie has a crunchy pecan topping & a smooth, spicy middle — good hot or cold; try it for Thanksgiving.

1 9 in. homemade pie shell	3 beaten eggs
½ c. chopped pecans	1 tsp. vanilla
2 c. cooked sweet potatoes	⅓ c. sugar
6 Tbsp. softened butter	1 tsp. cinnamon
¼ c. heavy cream	½ tsp. nutmeg

Preheat oven to 475°. Make your favorite pie shell — prick all over with fork & spread pecans in bottom. Bake 5 min. Cool. Lower heat to 300°. Mash together potatoes & butter till smooth. Add all other ingredients & blend well. Pour into pie shell. Make the

Topping

3 Tbsp. melted butter	½ c. brown sugar
⅔ c. pecans, finely chopped	⅓ c. flour

Combine all ingredients till crumbly. Sprinkle over top of pie. Put the pie on a cookie sheet & bake at 300° for 25~30 min. till golden brown. Delicious with whipped cream or ice cream.

Tea

I am a tea drinker — I drink it every morning with honey & milk. I learned to drink it that way from my best friend Janet, & her English mom, Maisie. ♥

The first time I had a "real" English tea was in a beautiful old hotel in London. I walked into the large room with its high ceilings & ornate moldings, massive windows (the rain was coming down hard), a fire in the huge fireplace & yellow roses everywhere. There was a grand piano & wonderful music & silver trays of delicate sandwiches, scones & biscuits, tiny cream puffs, cakes, & Napoleons. And pots of steaming hot tea. I was quite impressed! 😮 *wow*

But when it's tea time at home I usually don't make too much of a fuss — I feel like it's more a time for very close friends & family, kind of casual. My friends know to just drop in when they can. We usually have a plain cake or some nut bread & butter & I do serve the tea in the good China cups — even when I'm alone; I try to pay attention to the moment. I find myself more inclined in the winter afternoons, when it gets dark so early & there's a fire burning.

And once a winter I have my girlfriends over for a morning tea. First we trek out to the woods for a walk — then we settle in for Potato Heaven (p. 68), sausages cooked in maple syrup, and my grandma's Nut Bread (p.149). I encourage everyone to wear their most comfortable clothes & bring their slippers — so it's very cozy & not fussy at all. In front of the fire we drink tea & talk. ♥

Tea time is usually at 4pm. — it's a little interlude in the day & a quiet tradition. Recipes? Turn the page...

TEATIME

"The height of luxury was reached in the
winter afternoons... lying in a tin bath
in front of a coal fire, drinking tea,
and eating well-buttered crumpets...."
♥ J. C. Masterman

ELAINE'S FAMOUS SUGAR COOKIES

325° Makes 7 dozen

A wonderful tea cookie — you can color the sugar for Christmas cookies. ♥ From my dear friend, Elaine Sullivan. ♥

1 c. butter, softened
1 c. powdered sugar
1 c. granulated sugar
2 eggs
1 c. salad oil
2 tsp. vanilla

1 tsp. grated lemon peel
4¼ c. flour
1 tsp. baking soda
1 tsp. cream of tartar
1 tsp. salt
plain or colored sugar

Cream butter & sugars; beat in eggs one at a time until light & fluffy. Beat in oil, vanilla & lemon peel. Combine dry ingredients & gradually add to sugar mixture, beating till well blended. Wrap in wax paper; chill several hours.

Preheat oven to 325°. Grease 2 cookie sheets. Divide dough into thirds (keep ⅓ out, refrigerate the rest till needed). Form heaping tsp. of dough into ball. Place on cookie sheet. Flatten to 2" diameter with bottom of glass dipped in sugar. Sprinkle with plain or colored sugar & bake 8~10 min. till lightly browned. Let stand on cookie sheet 2~3 min. before removing. ♥

"Every man's life is a fairy tale written by God's fingers."
♥ Hans Christian Andersen

144

POPPY SEED CAKE

350°

This is sort of a plain cake, which, I think, is the charm of it. ♥

½ c. poppy seed
1 c. milk
1½ c. sugar
½ c. butter, softened
pinch of salt

1 tsp. vanilla
2 c. flour
2 tsp. baking powder
4 egg whites
powdered sugar

Soak poppy seed in milk for 1 hour. Preheat oven to 350°. Cream sugar & butter thoroughly. Add poppy seed with milk, salt, & vanilla. Stir in flour & baking powder. Beat egg whites stiffly & fold in. Pour into well-greased tube pan & bake 1 hour. Cool, turn out & sift over a little powdered sugar. ♥

"Optimism: A cheerful frame of mind
that enables a tea kettle to sing though
in hot water up to its nose."
Anonymous

145

Apple Muffins
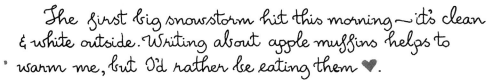

400° Makes 12

The first big snowstorm hit this morning — it's clean & white outside. Writing about apple muffins helps to warm me, but I'd rather be eating them ♥.

2 c. unbleached flour	1 c. peeled apple, chopped
3/4 tsp. salt	1/2 c. walnuts, chopped
4 tsp. baking powder	3/4 c. milk
1/4 c. sugar	2 eggs
1 tsp. cinnamon	cinnamon & 2 Tbsp. sugar
4 Tbsp. butter	12 apple rings, cored (use small apples)

Preheat oven to 400°. Mix together first 5 ingredients. Cut in butter with pastry blender. Add finely chopped apple & walnuts. Add milk to beaten eggs; stir into dry ingredients, just to moisten. Fill buttered muffin tins. Place an apple ring (unpeeled) on the top of each muffin & sprinkle tops with cinnamon mixed with 2 Tbsp. sugar to taste. Bake 20 min. Serve. ♥

"To Debbie Pookie Poople Pips from Petey Popsy Pooples — I love you — be mine."
♥ Valentine's message from the London Times, 1982

MAPLE PECAN SCONES

400° Makes 10

Heart-shaped, they look wonderful for tea, for breakfast, or even with soup. Serve with marmalade, butter & jam. ♥

2 c. flour
1 Tbsp. baking powder
¼ tsp. soda
¼ tsp. salt
4 Tbsp. cold sweet butter

½ c. ground pecans
⅓ c. cream
¼ c. maple syrup
1 whole egg
1 egg yolk

Preheat oven to 400°. Stir dry ingredients together with a fork. Chop the butter into bits & cut it into dry ingredients till it resembles coarse meal. Stir in pecans. Combine cream, maple syrup & egg. Stir into dry ingredients, just enough to hold together in a ball. Turn onto floured board; knead 30 seconds. Pat dough to ½" thick. Cut with floured 3" heart-shaped cutter. Mix the egg yolk with 1 Tbsp. water & brush tops of scones. Bake 1" apart on buttered cookie sheet for 15 min. till golden brown. Serve. ♥

TEA CAKES & HONEY BUTTER

350° Makes 16

Old-fashioned, hot little cakes — make them for someone you love.

1 c. hot milk
½ c. butter
1 tsp. salt
½ c. sugar
1 pkg. dry yeast
¼ c. warm water

3 eggs
3½ c. flour
⅓ c. sugar
1½ tsp. cinnamon
butter, softened
honey

Preheat oven to 350°. In a lg. bowl, pour hot milk over butter, salt, & sugar. Cool to lukewarm. Dissolve yeast in warm water; allow to stand 5 min. Add the yeast & eggs to milk mixture, beating well. Gradually add flour & beat till smooth. Cover with cloth, let rise in warm place 1 hour. Fill buttered muffin tins ½ full. Combine sugar & cinnamon; sprinkle 1 tsp. over each muffin. Bake 20-25 min. Cream softened butter with honey to taste & serve with the warm cakes.

"The little old kitchen had quieted down from the bustle and confusion of mid-day; and now, with its afternoon manners on, presented a holiday aspect, that as the principal room in the brown house, it was eminently proper it should have."

♥Margaret Sidney

NUT BREAD

325° Makes 1 loaf

Such an easy bread! No kneading or waiting—also, no fat! Makes a beautiful loaf of bread, nice with tea, & a sweet homey Christmas present. It comes with love from my Grandma, Florence "Spitfire" Orr Smith.

2 c. flour
2 tsp. baking powder
½ tsp. salt

⅓ c. sugar
1 egg, beaten
1 c. milk

½ c. walnuts, chopped

Preheat oven to 325°. Mix dry ingredients together with a fork. Beat the egg, mix it with milk & pour into dry ingredients. Mix well; stir in nuts. Pour into buttered bread pan; bake 35 min. till toothpick comes out dry. Serve with softened butter. ♥

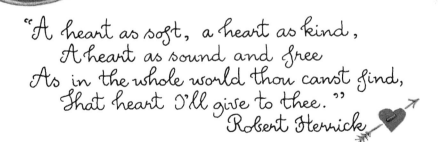

"A heart as soft, a heart as kind,
A heart as sound and free
As in the whole world thou canst find,
That heart I'll give to thee."
Robert Herrick

SANDWICHES

Use only the freshest of ingredients, the optimum in color, texture & flavor. For tea, crustless heart shapes, rounds & fingers look nice — you can arrange them on a paper doily if you like. If you are expecting weekend guests, a large platter of different sandwiches ready & waiting in the fridge comes in real handy. We never go to the beach without our cucumber sandwiches for sustenance. ♥

CUCUMBER : Cut rounds from good white bread, spread with mayonnaise, add thin slices peeled cucumber, salt & pepper. Spread sandwich edge with the thinnest coat of mayonnaise & roll edge in minced parsley. Chill. ♥

TOMATO: On fresh pumpernickel rounds, spread mayonnaise, add thin slices cherry tomato, salt & pepper, then fresh basil leaves. Chill. ♥

AVOCADO: Toast one side crustless wheat bread — spread mayonnaise on untoasted side, add avocado, pepper & salt, then sprouts. Cut into squares. Serve P.D.Q. ♥

NASTURTIUM: Spread white bread heart shapes with cream cheese, add fresh nasturtiums. ♥

RADISH: Slice French bread baguette, spread with sweet butter, add thick slices radish, pepper & serve open-faced. ♥

SANDWICHES

NOTE: For a baby shower, your bakery will add food coloring to bread, making it pink or blue. ♥ Looks terrible ♥, tastes just fine & certainly is festive. For Christmas buffet, do red & green.

CHICKEN: Finely chop cooked chicken, celery, walnuts. Mix with mayonnaise, add a bit of curry to taste. Spread on good white bread cut into finger shapes. Chill. ♥

CHEESE: Sharp cheddar on white bread with mustard & sliced sweet pickles. ♥

PEANUT BUTTER & JELLY: I like "extra crunchy" & lots of jelly. These should be heart-shaped & on white bread. ♥

HAPPY BIRTHDAY!

As the oldest of 8 children I have memories of many wonderful birthday parties. I think my mom must be the all-time expert on how to make a birthday special but then she made every day special for us ♥. On rainy days she'd let us turn the entire house into an underground maze of a tent ~ with the use of blankets, clothespins & various pieces of furniture we would have a castle. The only room that was off-limits was the kitchen, where on cold mornings she would close all the doors, turn on the oven to heat the room & fill the basinet with warm water in which she'd bathe "our" baby. It was cozy-warm & my little brother or sister was always fat & pink & slippery. I loved to help ~ my mom & I played "dolls" together with real babies ♥.

For birthday parties she would make wonderful creative cakes ~ sometimes we'd find dimes inside but my favorite was the "Circus Cake." It had candy canes stuck in the top holding up a pointed construction paper "roof" and animal crackers pressed into the pink frosting all around the sides. The whole thing was sprinkled with colored candies & we thought our mom was a genius. ♥

Here are some other birthday suggestions:

Sparklers make the cake look wonderful for your adult friends ~ no candles for unpleasant reminders! Don't forget to turn off the lights & sing LOUD.

Tuck something special ~ even just a little note ~ into lunchbox, briefcase, pockets or purse. ♥

DAD Birthday banners are fun ~ put them up along the travel route of the honored one. Say things like "Smile, Janet! It's your Birthday!!" ♥

Try a "Backwards Party." Everyone wears his clothes backwards; the invitation must be read by holding it up to a mirror, and the meal should start with dessert. ♥

Balloons, banners, hats, noisemakers, special invitations, placecards, crepe paper twists, nutcups & confetti bring birthday smiles to children of all ages. ♥

Have a "treasure hunt" for your children. Hide peanuts all over the yard ~ give each child a bag with his name on it ~ give them about 10 minutes from the GO! Have a prize for whoever finds the most nuts. ♥

Every child should go home with a "prize." Have a grab bag with small wrapped toys, one for the boys & one for the girls. 🎁 Everyone should have a balloon, too. ♥

Don't forget to take lots of pictures. ♥

When you're out & about & you see some~ thing special that doesn't cost an arm & a leg ~ BUY it. You'll always have a stock of presents for emergencies. ♥

EPILOGUE

'Been writing & cooking a year now or more,
    and now that I'm finished, I'm ready to soar.
But lo & behold, ten pounds have appeared;
    my tummy looks fat & my rear end looks weird!
I'm planning a visit to old friends out west;
    wishing & hoping that I'll look my best.
So it's sit-ups & leg-lifts from now on for me
    and one thing I promise, I will guarantee
That the next book I write, the next book you see
    will be veggies & health food & mostly fat free! ❤

FRIENDS

"To get the full value
of a Joy
You must have Somebody
to divide it with."
Mark Twain ♥

Special thanks to the "Somebodies" who stood by me with encouragement, diversion, and love. To Valerie Reese, who cooked up a storm while I painted, & made sure it all came out all right with the use of measuring cups & spoons! ♥ To Randi Russell & her new baby, Raleigh, for the experiences we share. ♥ And, most of all, to Joe Hall, my handsome "6'2" Leo who can cook" for believing me when I promised that after this, I'll make dinner. ♥

And it wouldn't be right if I forgot to mention Man Cat, Girl Cat, & Wm. T. Aristocat (Bill) for their contributions: walking across my pages with kitty feet was only one of the ideas they had to "help." ♥

155

INDEX

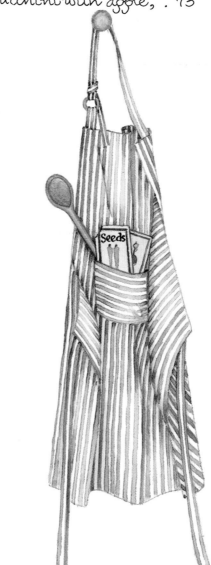
"Out of the strain of the Doing,
Into the race of the Done."
   ♥ Julia Woodruff